Praise for *Wh*

A captivating masterclass that provides a 360-degree view of exceptional leadership. Essential for current and aspiring principals, Couros and Apsey's work is filled with profound insights, actionable strategies, and heartfelt stories. With a deep appreciation for what's unique and dynamic in each of us, the authors offer a variety of approaches to inspire your own path. An absolute must-read, this book delivers the wisdom and guidance educational leaders have been waiting for!

—Lainie Rowell, bestselling author, award-winning educator, and international keynote speaker

What Makes a Great Principal dives into the essence of effective school leadership, highlighting five key pillars through real stories from teachers and students. This book is a heartfelt guide for educational leaders, offering practical strategies for making a real difference. It's an invaluable resource that looks at leadership through the eyes of those it impacts most, making it essential for any principal.

—Jerry Almendarez, superintendent

Bursting with empowering stories, this book showcases real-life principals who've left an indelible mark through relationship-building, collective efficacy, and authentic leadership. This book is designed for a principal's hectic schedule. It's a fun and enlightening read that can be picked up when you have a couple of minutes for inspiration. Dive into this treasure trove of wisdom and elevate your leadership to new heights.

—Michelle Krell, executive director, Minnesota Elementary School Principals' Association (MESPA)

This book brilliantly combines the personal and the practical. The personal stories are authentic, reflecting the personal experiences of the authors. The practical advice helps current and aspiring school leaders make deliberate choices about how to pursue the five pillars of effective leadership. Best of all, the book does not add more things for leaders to do but helps us know what to stop doing. If we don't connect with students, staff, and communities, nothing else matters. I hope district leaders will also read this book and ask if their next directive to principals is helping to create connections or interfering with relationships.

—**Douglas Reeves**, author, *Fearless Schools*

What Makes a Great Principal is a must-read for the novice or seasoned school principal. It provides readers with practical tools and lessons that make a good principal a great leader, based on five pillars of successful leadership. I highly recommend this as a guide for improvement and source of motivation.

—**Paul Liabenow,** executive director, Michigan Elementary and Middle School Principals Association

What Makes a Great Principal offers a clear roadmap to effective school leadership. What sets this book apart is its grounding in real-life stories and strategies shared by teachers and students directly impacted by exceptional leadership. Through compelling anecdotes and practical advice, the authors demonstrate how these pillars translate into action, fostering a positive school culture, promoting teacher development, and driving student success. By viewing school leadership through the eyes of those most affected by it, this book provides invaluable insights and inspiration for both aspiring and current school leaders, making it essential reading for anyone dedicated to improving education and their own leadership craft.

—**Jessica Gomez,** author, presenter, and district administrator

When I think of powerful examples of leadership, Allyson Apsey and George Couros are two names that always come to my mind. After reading *What Makes a Great Principal*, I'm even more convinced about how much I still have to learn in my own journey. There are so many powerful lessons throughout this book, with countless immediate takeaways. This is one of those books that I think every leader should read to become not only a better leader but also a better person.

—**Todd Nesloney,** director of Culture and Strategic Leadership, TEPSA

What Makes a Great Principal is the perfect resource for new administrators and veteran principals. If you are looking to up your game as a school principal or in any leadership role, this is the book for you! George Couros and Allyson Apsey know what it takes to successfully lead a school.

—**Glen Abshere,** executive director, Oklahoma Association of Elementary School Principals

What Makes a Great Principal

George Couros and Allyson Apsey

What Makes a Great
PRINCIPAL

The Five Pillars of
Effective School Leadership
—— STORIES FROM THE FIELD ——

What Makes a Great Principal: The Five Pillars of Effective School Leadership
© 2024 George Couros and Allyson Apsey

This book is available at special discounts when purchased in quantity for educational purposes or for use as premiums, promotions, or fundraisers. For inquiries and details, contact the publisher at books@impressbooks.org.

Published by IMPress, a division of Dave Burgess Consulting, Inc.
IMPressbooks.org

DaveBurgessConsulting.com
San Diego, CA

Paperback ISBN: 978-1-948334-73-0
Ebook ISBN: 978-1-948334-74-7

Cover and interior design by Liz Schreiter
Edited and produced by Reading List Editorial
ReadingListEditorial.com

This book is lovingly dedicated to two extraordinary groups of individuals: current or aspiring principals and their families.

To current or aspiring principals: The future of education is in your capable and powerful hands. We are thrilled to be able to partner with you to focus on the five pillars of great principals. Through a blend of research and stories from you and those you lead, we can gain inspiration and insights, and formulate actionable steps to lead schools that truly embody what our students deserve. In these challenging times, your leadership is more crucial than ever, and we extend our deepest gratitude for your unwavering dedication and sacrifices.

To the families of current or aspiring principals: Your indispensable support is the cornerstone of successful leadership. We understand that leaders are not the sole bearers of sacrifices. You endure their boundless passion for education, embrace the late nights, navigate them through moments of self-doubt, and stand as their constant support. Both of us, drawing from personal experience, acknowledge that our leadership journeys would be incomplete without the steadfast support of our families.

From George: Thank you to my parents for teaching me that leadership is about serving others and bringing joy to the world each day. To my children, Marino, Georgia, and Kallea, who inspire me with their curiosity and enthusiasm. And to my wonderful wife, Paige, who not only supports and encourages me to take on new personal and professional projects but somehow juggles being the best mom (tied with Allyson) and a publishing company CEO at the same time.

From Allyson: I am grateful to my parents for teaching me that I belong anywhere I want to be, even at the head of the table. Thank you to my husband, Jim, for believing in me even when I don't believe in myself. Thank you to my sons, Laine and Tyson, for giving me the best job in the world—being your mom. I love you to the moon and back, and setting an example for you is my biggest goal in life.

CONTENTS

INTRODUCTION

BY GEORGE COUROS

Do schools need principals?

I remember that this was a question being asked on social media by teachers back in 2015, and there were many conversations on why principals were not beneficial to a school community and perhaps even caused more problems than they solved.

A good friend of mine wrote a blog post on the topic, emphatically saying that a school could continue to exist without a principal and may in fact even benefit from their absence.

Now, in the history of education, has a school without a principal persevered and accelerated due to this reality?

Probably.

I called my friend after I read his post, and I remember saying to him, "You probably wrote that post not because you think schools would be better off without a principal but because you have never had a really good one."

Was I bothered by this conversation on social media and by the post from my friend? Definitely. But it was not just because I was a principal at the time. It was because I had a great principal who not only altered the trajectory of my career but, I could honestly say, my life. That one person changed everything.

What Is the Difference between a Leader and an Administrator?

For the past few years and at the time of writing this book, I have been asking people within education the question "Who is a great administrator you have worked with, and what made them great?" Unfortunately, too many times people can't think of one. It is an awkward moment, but there are lessons to be learned from their lack of response.

But on the opposite end of the spectrum, a common theme emerges in the responses from the educators I have asked over the years about the best leaders they have experienced: "They brought out and saw something that I had no idea was in me."

Notice that I ask the question "What makes a great administrator?" not "What makes a great leader?"

Those are two very different questions.

Some administrators are terrible leaders, and other people who aren't administrators become unofficial leaders in moving their communities forward in a positive manner.

If you think of the best teachers you have had in your lifetime, you might say the same thing you said about administrators: "They brought out and saw something in me that I had no idea was in me."

Some of the traits of the best teachers and best principals are the same.

In fact, when the term *leader* is used in this book, it is not synonymous with *administrator* or *principal*. We define the term *leader* in the following manner: a leader is someone who has the ability to move people forward in a positive direction.

And as much as we would love to talk about what makes a great leader, no matter the role, this book is focused specifically on what makes a principal a great leader.

Although any administrator, or anyone who aspires to be in that position, will benefit from what we share in this book, we wanted to focus on the role of the principal.

I remember Todd Whitaker saying at a conference, "When the principal sneezes, the whole school gets a cold."[1] That couldn't be more true.

But what is the opposite of that statement?

"When the principal takes Sudafed, the whole school no longer suffers from nighttime sniffles, coughing, and aches?"

It just doesn't have the same ring.

(P.S. Sudafed did not pay us for the product placement. #NotAnAd)

As someone who refereed high-level basketball, I often think of the connection between that role and being a principal. In any sport, you know a referee is great when you don't notice them. They not only lead, but they manage the game so well, and everything goes in a positive direction where the focus is on the game, not the official. It doesn't mean there isn't adversity, but the best officials know how to deal with it in a way where the focus is where it should be: on the players and the game.

Unfortunately, if you are a bad referee, everyone notices. Like, *everyone*.

The same is true for principals.

The worst ones stick out, and the best ones never get the credit for the impact they have on the little and big things in our schools. They often take the criticism for others and hand out the praise when they might be the most deserving.

No great principal has ever won an award and pulled a Snoop Dogg in an awards ceremony and said, "And most importantly, I would like to thank me!" As much as that statement could be true, they know that they are a large part of the success of the community, but their success is a direct result of the success of their community.

There is no better person that I could think of who exemplifies this than my former principal, Kelly Wilkins.

There's Just Something About Kelly

For over the past decade, I have written or cowritten four books and two thousand blog posts, and recorded or been a guest on over five hundred podcasts.

All of this content could have been titled, "Everything I Ever Learned about Education I Learned from Kelly Wilkins." She has been the biggest inspiration in my career, and when I met her, not only did my career change, but so did my life.

I can honestly say that I never thought much about principals and their role until Kelly came into my life. I really didn't think of the position more than that—it was just a position in the school. And sometimes you don't realize your former principals weren't that great until you get a principal who is exemplary.

Kelly was that for me.

The Best Way to Cultivate the Best Talent Is to Find Talented People

My first interaction with Kelly was in an interview for a position at the school where she was principal. This was a brand-new school, only in its second year of existence, and Kelly was charged with opening it and setting the course for the community.

I remember when applying for the position that it was a unique posting. It wasn't for a specific grade level or subject area. It was for a grade 5–9 teacher. Of course, there were some job requirements posted, but it was really just a general posting with little information.

At the time that job was posted, I knew I needed a change, and I wasn't happy in my current situation. Not because it was a bad school or community, but I just felt I had lost my purpose. Teaching was something I did but not something I was passionate about. I threw in an application, got an interview, and was so excited about the opportunity.

As I entered the interview room, Kelly and the assistant principal, Carolyn Cameron (who also went on to be a *great* principal later in her career), had a list of fifteen topics on a piece of paper. They told me to look the list over for a few minutes and then talk about five to eight things listed that I was passionate about. That was a strange process and very different from the question-and-answer interview format that I was used to not only as a teacher but in every profession. Something already felt different.

I wish I could tell you great details about that interview, but it was a blur. I remember laughing, crying (not kidding), and really feeling passionate about what I shared. It felt like having coffee with good friends or colleagues more than an interview, which was the point. If you think of the typical interview process, it feels more like an inquisition than a conversation.

When I left the interview, I felt good about it, but it was unlike anything I had ever experienced in my career, so I had no idea how to gauge how well I did.

A few days later, Kelly called me and not only offered me the job but also shared what my position would be.

It was to teach the subjects that *I* was really good at and was most passionate about. The job was literally tailored to who I was, my strengths and my passions. What I thought was just pure luck was actually very planned out. Kelly looked for the best people she could find and then figured out how we could match the best person possible (and their skills) with the needs of the school culture. You see, when you are looking for the best grade 5 math teacher, you might be giving up on the *best* teacher possible for your community because you advertised for a very specific position. Not only did you probably deter people who would be great for your community, but you have made the job so specific that your hands are tied in the process.

Kelly felt I was the best fit for the school community, and then she collaborated with her team to figure out how they could switch things up in their school and bring me in. When she offered me the job and told me about the position, I enthusiastically accepted. She asked me to keep it private because she wanted to let the other candidates know they didn't get the job and give them feedback to help them in the future. Kelly knew that any person in that process would probably teach students *somewhere*, and she wanted to set up the people who were unsuccessful in the interview to find success in another school.

A few days later, I signed the contract, and I couldn't have been more excited.

Relationships and the Importance of Feeling Valued

What was interesting was that I was really excited about this opportunity at a new school with Kelly, but just a month earlier, I'd been ready to leave education. I felt I had lost my passion, and this new school was a last-ditch effort to give it one more go. To be honest, I probably wouldn't have even applied, but I wasn't sure what else I would do.

Within days of signing the contract, I received a call to interview for a job outside of a school, with a focus on educational technology at the office of education in my province. To say that this was a dream job for me would be an understatement. It was exactly the job I was hoping for, and I couldn't believe the timing. For years I'd tried to get this interview, with no luck. Then right when I sign a contract, an opportunity becomes available. It was like the ex-partner who broke your heart and then reaches out just when you've finally forgotten them! Oh, the torment!

I knew I had to take the interview, but how could I do that within days of signing a contract? In my mind I had two choices: take the interview without telling Kelly, who was really a stranger to me at this time, or tell Kelly about the opportunity and hope that I didn't get fired from a job I hadn't even started.

I decided to go with the latter decision. Kelly had been so welcoming to me that I felt I owed her the truth. I dialed her number, feeling like Eminem in a rap battle in the movie *8 Mile* (without the mom's spaghetti). She picked up. I reluctantly told her that I'd been offered an interview, and I wanted to tell her before accepting it as a courtesy.

I will never forget what she said: "George, if this is your dream job, you have to take the interview. If you get it, we will be bummed for us but happy for you. We will find someone else to work here. But if you don't get it, we will be really excited about the opportunity to work with you. I would never want you wondering 'what if?' and resenting your decision if you didn't take that interview and hated being here because of it. I promise you either way we will be good."

It wasn't just what she said but also how she said it.

I felt so amazingly valued, and there is a huge difference between *being* valued and *feeling* valued.

What an incredible feeling to know you are valued as a person who has hopes and dreams, and to have someone who truly has your back, no matter your decision. If this is how I was treated before I worked there, I couldn't imagine how good it would be once I did.

> There is a huge difference between *being* valued and *feeling* valued.

Suddenly, a third option appeared. I didn't even take the interview. I knew where I wanted to be.

Being Visionary through Understanding What We Can Do Together

As I entered this new school, the opportunities seemed endless, which was something I had not really experienced. It just felt different.

Then I got my schedule.

Part of it was teaching middle school math in a collaborative setting. That was something I was excited about.

But the other half was being an educational technology facilitator who would work directly with teachers in a team situation, where we could open up opportunities for students through a collaborative process.

That was exciting. But how it was scheduled, not so much.

Kelly provided a schedule that had times for me to work with the math classes and then forty-minute blocks when I would work with individual teachers and their class once a week. It was seen as an opportunity to spread my strengths around to the staff, but the first thing I thought was, *How can I possibly get anything moving forward in such a short window of time each week?* It would be hard to build not only a connection with each class but momentum. Although this was similar to what I had done in the past with other schools, it didn't mean that it made sense. My mom always told me that if you want something, ask for it, and the worst you might hear is no. Ninety-nine percent of the time I would agree with her, but having a temporary contract, I thought this might be the exception. I decided to ask Kelly anyway.

Kelly and I met, and she asked for my thoughts on the schedule before I was ready to share them. She knew something was up. I told her that I thought it didn't really make sense to do forty-minute blocks with classes once a week, and I thought there could be a better way. Of course, when you say there is a better way, you might expect for someone to ask, "Well, what is it?" Kelly asked, but I wasn't prepared yet with an answer. I thought I would share my concerns, and she would either say no or fix it. I didn't think my input would be requested.

One thing I know is that if you complain about a problem, when you are done complaining, it is still a problem. Only action creates solutions.

Kelly said to me, "Go think about it, and see if you can come up with a better way."

Huh? That was new!

I came back a week later and said, "Would it be possible for me to just work with one class for two to three weeks at a time and do some deep, project-based work? I promise you that I will work with the teachers and classes the same amount, but instead of once a week, it would be every day for a couple of weeks at a time, and then I would rejoin them for another two- or three-week block later in the year."

She loved it and said, "Go for it!"

What weird, utopian school is this where I have input on my schedule as a teacher on a temporary contract, who hasn't even taught a classroom for a solitary second?

Leaders need to be visionary, but they need to also be able to utilize the people they work with to create a vision of what school *should* and *could* be together. We often see vision as something that one person has, not something that is created together.

> **Leaders need to be visionary, but they need to also be able to utilize the people they work with to create a vision of what school *should* and *could* be together.**

Kelly knew her strengths and my strengths. Together, we could create something together that we couldn't do alone.

Maximizing Resources through Genuine Ownership of the Outcome

When I tell you that this was the best year of teaching I had ever had, that would be an understatement. I often tell educators that we need to look forward and create the school of our dreams by looking back at our intentions when we first started. We often blame the "system" for wearing people down, but the "system" is made up of people, and if that is true, I can have an impact, and so can my principal.

As the year neared its end, Kelly asked to meet with me to discuss the opportunities for the following year. She brought me in and said,

"Hey, George, we have this money in our budget for technology next year, and I want you to write up a plan of how we are going to use it."

I looked at her, confused, and said, "I don't think that is my job. Isn't that something you should do?" In my entire career as a teacher, I had *never* been asked by the principal how we should spend money for the entirety of the school.

Kelly returned the confused look and said, "George, we hired you as the expert in educational technology for the school, so why would *we* make that decision when *you* have the expertise? This is part of the reason we hired you."

You know when people say, "There are no dumb questions"? Typically, that is said after someone asks a dumb question.

The weird thing is that, with Kelly, I realized that I had just asked the dumb question. "Isn't that something you should do?" made no sense in her world, as we were a team and decisions were made together, utilizing the expertise of the entire school community.

I went off and worked on a plan for what we were going to purchase for the school, utilizing the budget I was allocated.

Do you know how much pressure there is when you are making decisions as a teacher that will impact other teachers?

I didn't want them complaining about the terrible technology choices they had access to when I was the one making the decision! So instead of making the decision on my own, I started asking other teachers their thoughts and hopes for what they could utilize in their classrooms. Some had amazing ideas, and some needed guidance. But they all appreciated me asking.

I came back with a plan, and I will tell you, I was terrified. Kelly put me in a position where I was making decisions for others in my role, and it gave me more ownership over the entirety of the school, not just the classes I taught. She knew that how money was spent on "stuff" would either benefit or hinder the school, so she would defer to the experts. This was the first time in my teaching career where I felt like I was considered an "expert" in my own school. Maximizing resources isn't just about making decisions on what you purchase and how you utilize time; it is maximizing the people you serve to do that together.

You can have all the vision in the world, but it doesn't matter much when you don't have the resources to bring these dreams to fruition.

Once You Stop Learning, You Are Done Teaching

When I tell you that was the best year of teaching in my life, it was not because, under Kelly's guidance, things started going downhill in year two. It was because I never made it to year two in that school.

Remember, a year earlier, I'd been ready to quit teaching. The summer after my first year working with Kelly, it was because of Kelly's coaxing that I accepted a job as an assistant principal at a school in the district. Not only did I stay in the profession, but I doubled down and became an administrator. Because of Kelly, I can't imagine being involved with any other profession to this day.

We often talk about how we live in an incredible time where we have access to all the information in the world. Although I would agree, it is much more powerful that we have access to one another. After I took a position at another school, Kelly never hesitated to reach out to me and ask me for advice in areas she knew I was well versed in. Kelly never looked at someone's position as a measure of their knowledge and wisdom. She was so incredibly ahead of her time because she was willing to learn from anyone and everyone, and she surrounded herself with the best.

I remember sitting in a leadership meeting as an assistant principal when a group of longtime principals started joking with Kelly about me leaving her school so soon, and how she couldn't keep anyone on her staff.

Her response was a mic drop.

She looked at them and said, "I would rather have someone amazing for one year in my school than have someone who is average for ten."

She looked for the best people she could find and learn from, and if she helped them go to other positions, she knew she could find different people who would want to come work with her. Wouldn't you want your boss to bring out the best in you, even if that meant you would eventually leave?

Kelly's legacy was in the people who were all over the region because of her direct influence on the acceleration of their careers, and they were loyal to her for that. If she called you, you would always answer. She knew who to go to for what and how to utilize their gifts to grow her own.

She eventually became the deputy superintendent of the district and remained in that position until she retired. Never once did I ask her a question where she pretended she knew the answer. She either knew how to guide you, or she would say, "That is a great question. Give me some time, and let me see if I can get you an answer." She always got me an answer or knew someone who could help me.

When I became a principal, I knew I didn't need to know everything, but I had to be willing to learn anything that could help the people I served. There was no better example of this than Kelly, and her influence lives on in me today. If I could make one-tenth of the impact Kelly made in her career, I would consider myself a success.

From the Viewpoint of Those You Serve

A question I have been asking teachers forever is, "Would you want to be a learner in your own classroom?" Some hear that question, are a bit offended, and adamantly, immediately answer, "Yes!"

It is not intended to be a one-and-done question but something we think about constantly and try to understand from the viewpoint of those we serve. I fully admit I have had bad days as a teacher, for instance, those days I said, "The bell doesn't dismiss you; I dismiss you!" Those were the days I sucked. Kids were literally bolting for the door to get out of my classroom as soon as possible those days.

Yet on other days, they didn't even notice the time because they felt so interested and empowered in their learning. That was the goal, and to achieve it as much as possible is the standard.

When I shared the above question in a talk, a teacher said to me, "This is also something a principal should consider. 'Would I want to be a staff member in my own community?'"

She was right. And that moment is one of the reasons we felt it was so essential to have staff and student voices represented extensively throughout the book. You can learn a lot from people doing your same job, but never neglect learning from the people under your care.

So as you read this book, think about what principals you've worked for have done, but also consider the principal you wished you had when you were a teacher. Too often I ask some teachers with incredible leadership potential if they have ever considered becoming a principal, and they will say, "I don't want to do the things a principal does."

To which I respond, "When you are the principal, you can do it the way you want to do it. That's the beauty of the job!"

Obviously there are certain requirements of the job, but there is also considerable flexibility. People tell me they would miss kids too much being a principal, to which I respond that I was around kids *all the time* because I made it an integral part of my day.

As you read on, think of these two questions: Who is the principal I want to be, and who is the principal my community needs?

If the answers to those questions are in the back of your mind as you read the ideas, research, and stories ahead, you have all the potential to be a great principal.

> # Who is the principal I want to be, and who is the principal my community needs?

That is the goal of this book.

So . . . do schools need principals?

Not necessarily.

But would schools and people benefit tremendously from having a great principal? Absolutely.

I remember talking to that same friend who wrote that post on why schools didn't need principals a few years later, and he had a different attitude. A new principal had come to his community, and it changed everything.

In my personal experience, I was lucky enough to enter a school that already had a great principal, and if it weren't for my job change, I probably could have written the same post my friend did. But when a great principal enters a new community, every person gets a fresh start, but they also get a better start.

I wanted to write this book with Allyson not because I was a great principal but because I had one.

And it made all the difference in the world to me, my colleagues, the community, and, mostly, the students.

3 QUESTIONS FOR CONVERSATION AND REFLECTION

1   Who was the best principal you have had, and why do you believe that?

2   As a principal or aspiring principal, what is one idea from the stories about Kelly that you would like to try and/or modify in your practice?

3   This is not a question, but if you have had a great principal, reach out to them and tell them. Too often, we only hear the complaints and not the compliments.

What Makes a Great Principal: The Five Pillars

BY ALLYSON APSEY

Before I say anything at all in this book, I want to say this: I loved being a principal. So much so that I stayed in the position for nineteen years and was a principal of all school levels. As George and I collaborated on this book, we both revisited how much we loved the role of principal. That is not to say it does not have its challenges, and I lived through some of the most challenging times to be a principal as we navigated a global pandemic. For me and for George, the rewards always made the challenges worth it. And, as a bonus, we can become better leaders through every challenge. We didn't get into school leadership to be good. We got into this profession to be great. So, let's dive into what makes a great principal.

> **We didn't get into school leadership to be good. We got into this profession to be great.**

Educators tend to have a love-hate relationship with research.

When the research supports our current thinking, we love it. When it doesn't, well . . . it can be hard to understand. And as contexts change, we have to question whether or not the research fits the goal of where we are now and where we are trying to go, not perpetuating the school models that have worked for a different era. The reality is that we can find research out there to support just about any line of thinking. But is it valid research? In his book *Fearless Schools*, Dr. Douglas Reeves talks about looking for a "preponderance of evidence" in research that points all in the same direction.[2] We have that with school leadership; most of the research supports similar effective leadership characteristics. Here's the deal, though. In the actual day-to-day life of a principal, our time is consumed with putting out fires, managing logistics, responding to emails, and other duties-as-assigned. The leadership behaviors that positively impact student success are way too often left unchecked on the to-do list at the end of the day. This is not because principals don't want to support the achievement of their students in every way they can; it is because they are pulled in every direction under the sun and are not able to prioritize the most important work in school leadership.

No pressure, school leaders, but research says that student success banks on your effectiveness. George shared how one great principal can change the life of a teacher or student forever, and research supports that thinking. A principal can accelerate student achievement up to seven months in a single year, or lower student achievement by up to seven months, depending on how effective the principal is, according to a 2013 study by Gregory F. Branch, Eric A. Hanushek, and Steven G. Rivkin.

> Our results indicate that highly effective principals raise the achievement of a typical student in their schools by between two and seven months of learning in a single school year; ineffective principals lower achievement by the same amount. These impacts are somewhat smaller than those associated with having a highly effective teacher. But teachers have a direct impact on only those students in

their classroom; differences in principal quality affect all students in a given school.[3]

We know how impactful a school principal is, and the problem with many of the studies that point to the correlation of effective principals and student achievement is that they often do not define the specific characteristics that make a principal effective. To answer the question "What makes a great principal?" we gathered evidence from scholarly research and experience from practitioners and shaped the five pillars to guide us in defining what makes a great principal.

These are the five pillars:

1. Relationship Builder
2. Continuous Learner
3. Talent Cultivator
4. Resource Maximizer
5. Visionary

In this book, we will share why these pillars matter, along with insights, strategies, and stories from both former and current principals who embody them, and also from teachers and students who have directly benefited from the impact of a great principal. The pillars of a great principal don't create a nice, neat acronym, which is often how we do things in education to make them more memorable, whether they are valid or not. Believe me, if everything you need to be a leader is actually in the acronym *LEADER*, then someone was trying to fit letters to ideas first, to make something catchy rather than good. (There are lots of diseases that are catchy, and I still don't want anything to do with them.) We wanted this book to be different in the sense that most of what you'll learn comes directly from people who served in the position or from those who directly benefited from someone who was a great principal.

The five pillars are discussed individually in this book, but we understand that these practices are interconnected. For instance, teachers would not feel supported without the necessary tools to do their job, so being a Resource Maximizer is essential. However, being a relationship-focused principal is integral to every single one of the pillars above. Being there for staff, students, and families; listening with an open mind; demonstrating empathy and understanding; developing trust; and being physically present are all woven into prioritizing relationships. If a leader does not connect with staff, students, or the school community, there is a very slim chance that any of the other characteristics of an effective principal will matter much. We know that children don't learn from teachers they don't respect, and the same is true for principals and staff.

Here is a table we created for your use as you reflect on the pillars throughout the book. You can also find this and other resources at whatmakesagreatprincipal.com.

PERSONAL / TEACHER REFLECTION			
Core Pillar	What does each core pillar look like in my work and growth as an administrator?	What are some examples of what this looks like in my school? What could it look like?	How will I know that this pillar is having a positive impact on the school community?
Relationship Builder			
Continuous Learner			
Talent Cultivator			
Resource Maximizer			
Visionary			

PILLAR ONE

Relationship Builder

Great principals understand that strong, positive relationships are foundational to the success of their school, and they are constantly looking for ways to support relationships throughout the environment. Effective principals model the empathy, joy, and connection needed for positive relationships among staff, students, and families in the school community. They know that every interaction matters and model that every day.

PREFACE
Key to Greatness

BY GEORGE COUROS

Human interaction is the key force in overcoming resistance and speeding change.

—ATUL GAWANDE

As a principal in Northern Canada, we had some really cold days (we are talking minus 40, which is the same in Celsius *and* Fahrenheit, so everyone understands how cold that is), but it didn't matter. As a principal, I was outside greeting students, staff, and community members every day. Where did I learn this from? My mom, who would stand at the front of the restaurant and greet people as they entered each evening. Her mentality was that this was not just about food, it was about the experience that people had on the nights they chose to be in our small family restaurant. What is the experience people have as they enter your school?

Also, every day, I would do my best to see every student and staff member in the school, even if it was for thirty seconds to say something like, "It is so good to see you today; thank you for being here." That simple acknowledgment was meaningful to our community. You might also see me come into a classroom, wreak havoc for a few seconds to rile kids up, and leave them to the teacher.

And why on earth would I do that? Because school should be a joyous place. As a subtle reminder, school might be the most joyous place not only for some students but also for some of the adults in the building. We should never take that for granted.

Where did I pick this up from? My dad. He used to work in the back kitchen, then come out and check on people to see how they were doing and how their food was that evening. He understood this: without the customer, there is no restaurant. Without the students, there is no school. It always reminded me to ask the question "Who serves whom?"

I share this all with you because, as a beginning principal, I was given much grace in the mistakes I made and personal growth that I needed (and still do). I knew that if people saw who I was there for, they would be more patient.

One of the best principals I have ever worked with was Dr. David Pysyk. I honestly have never met a principal who was more universally loved than him, and it was almost scary how much people respected and appreciated him.

He shared with me once that a teacher who is great with relationships but bad with curriculum can last a lot longer than one who is the opposite. I will never forget that statement because of how simple yet true it seemed to be.

The same is true with principals.

The Key to Everything

Although this preface is meant to set the table for the pillar of Relationship Builder, this is also a reminder that none of the other domains matters if you aren't effective in this area.

Want to develop talent in your building? You have to build relationships.

Want to maximize how you utilize resources in your school? You have to know your people.

Want to create a compelling vision for your community? Do it with them.

Want to continuously grow in your learning? Know who you serve and how your growth can best help them.

Specifically that last point.

Associate superintendent of Katy ISD Sanée Bell wrote this in her book, *Be Excellent on Purpose*, and it has always resonated with me:

> Students should have rich, relevant, and authentic experiences at school, across the board. If every educator in every school pursued excellence instead of allowing excuses about what students can and cannot do, we would meet the needs of all students. Our goal has to be to create schools where excellence is the standard.[4]

> **You can be taught the day-to-day process of an organization, but no one can teach you to care about the people you serve.**

When you read this passage, where would being a relationship builder not be crucial?

A principal who is great with relationships and weak at administration will last longer than the other way around. You can be taught the day-to-day process of an organization, but no one can teach you to care about the people you serve. Every other pillar in this book is ultimately served by this one.

Don't Forget about the Relationship with Those Outside of School

As you read the chapters ahead from the people who benefited tremendously from a principal's ability to build relationships, please note that this was the *easiest* domain to compile stories about to share with you all. In fact, as you read about the other pillars, you will see that relationships are vital to the success of the teacher and the student.

It is important to remember that although relationships are crucial in our school communities, they are just as important outside of them. Too often, great principals become struggling people because they give everything to their school and have nothing left for their family, friends, and, most often, themselves. It is easy to give everything to everyone else and have nothing left over for ourselves.

The weird thing is that when we regularly take care of ourselves, it leads to better leadership. This quote from musician Solange Knowles is a truth many principals, current and past, could attest to: "When you take care of yourself, you're a better person for others. When you feel good about yourself, you treat others better."

Do you want your students and staff to be burned-out and have no lives outside of school? Of course not. So understand they are following your actions more than your words.

Subtle remarks in what we hear in education speak to the opposite message and can set a tone that school is everything and we must give up our personal lives for the sake of education. This is one of the reasons I prefer that we refer to schools as a team, not family.

To encapsulate this point, I'll share a quote from the 2014 *Harvard Business Review* article "Your Company Is Not a Family," in which the authors point out how differently we treat our own children when things are not going well, versus someone in our organization:

> In a real family, parents can't fire their children. Try to imagine disowning your child for poor performance:

"We're sorry Susie, but your mom and I have decided you're just not a good fit. Your table-setting effort has been deteriorating for the past 6 months, and your obsession with ponies just isn't adding any value. We're going to have to let you go. But don't take it the wrong way; it's just family."[5]

You can't do everything for everyone, nor would you want to. As you focus on building relationships in your community, realize the ones that are often not mentioned in schools are the ones that will be the most important long after you serve in the role.

Moving Forward

Being a relationship builder is the fastest way to get things done in your organization. As Reverend Jennifer Bailey shares, "Relationships are built at the speed of trust, and social change happens at the speed of relationships." If a student is sent to your office, the worst way to start off the interaction is by saying, "What is your name again?" If you want a teacher to try something new, building on her strengths is a much better approach than tearing her down. If you want parents to support your goals, you have to make time to get to know theirs. The time you take to build relationships in your staff, students, community, and outside of school is an investment you will get back tenfold. Not only does it save time eventually, but it can impact the people you serve long after their time in your community.

CHAPTER 1

Relationship Builder

BY ALLYSON APSEY

> There is a difference between being a leader and being a boss. Both are based on authority. A boss demands blind obedience; a leader earns his authority through understanding and trust.
>
> —KLAUS BALKENHOL

Trusting relationships are rooted in the knowledge that *everyone* is doing the best they can at the time, with the information and skills they have. Everyone includes teachers, support staff, students, families, and leaders. Principals cannot do this work alone, nor should they. It is crucial that all adults in the school are committed to developing relationships that empower others to do the hard work of being educators in the most effective way possible. There is an abundance of research that supports the idea that feeling connected and socially fulfilled leads to better outcomes. BetterUp, a comprehensive coaching organization, conducted research to analyze the role of belonging at work, both in terms of the benefits when belonging is present and the negative impact of a lack of belonging. None of us will be surprised to hear that their research showed there are significant positive outcomes when staff members feel a sense of belonging, and there are many significant negative impacts when they don't. But how would you like to reduce the number of sick days that employees take by 75 percent? According to BetterUp's research, organizations can dramatically reduce sick days by helping every single employee feel like they belong—that they are seen, valued, and appreciated.[6] This makes so much sense at schools, that when teachers and staff members feel a deep sense of belonging because they are seen for their special talents and skills, they are happier and healthier and want to be there.

> **When teachers and staff members feel a deep sense of belonging because they are seen for their special talents and skills, they are happier and healthier and want to be there.**

As he shares in his book *The Happiness Advantage*, Shawn Achor found that success doesn't lead to happiness, but instead happiness leads to success. There is no way the achievement problems in our schools will be corrected until the environmental problems in our schools are corrected. We know that the need for belonging and positive relationships is important for students too. And, of course, there is research to support that as well. In fact, R. Allan Allday and Kerri Pakurar found that the simple act of greeting students by name and with a positive comment at the classroom door increases on-task behavior by as much as 40 percent.[7]

This is further evidence that teachers and students must feel connected and fulfilled in order to do their best work.

There are some relationship-building basics that each leader can apply right away.

1. **Toss out your desk chair.** Like many other principals, I used this strategy to get in and out of my office as quickly as possible. Remarkably, every time I was away from my office and out and about in the school, I was at the right place at the right time. I better understood the strengths and challenges that staff members and students were encountering. I was able to promote teacher leadership on the spot by connecting teachers to share their strengths with each other. I was able to help out in important moments when teachers really needed a hand . . . like when they needed a quick bathroom break. Or when they needed a hand on the shoulder and a reminder of all the gifts they bring to the school. Or when they needed a sounding board, and I would rather it be me than anyone else because of the valuable perspective it gave me and the valuable perspective I could offer the teacher.

2. **Apply the power of accurate estimates of teacher achievement.** Like many of you, I am a huge fan of John Hattie's work. One of the reasons I appreciate his effect size work so much is because it is a synthesis of different meta-analyses that provides that "preponderance of evidence" that Doug Reeves talks about. A portion of his research addresses the power of accurate estimates of student achievement. He found that having accurate estimates of student achievement can supercharge student growth. This makes perfect sense because when teachers know exactly where students are with their achievement and what their next steps are, they can target the exact instruction students need. Hattie says, "The best information about student achievement is their achievement, and if this is underestimated or students are not working to their optimal, this can create a self-fulfilling prophecy."[8] Let's take this same idea and apply it to principal estimates of teacher achievement. Leaders need to be crystal clear about individual teacher strengths and communicate those strengths

to the teachers. From my experience, I see teacher strengths being continually underestimated, which results in teachers feeling undervalued and frustrated in their work. This is especially true when it comes to teacher evaluations. In my book *Leading the Whole Teacher*, I challenge principals to shift our thinking around the teacher evaluation to make it a teacher empowerment tool, with the sole purpose of supporting teachers to lean into their strengths. There is no better way to build relationships with teachers than to really know their strengths and make sure that they know you know.

3. **Have only one committee—the teacher happiness committee.** The best people to give input on creating a need-satisfying environment for teachers . . . are teachers. They can easily identify current strengths and areas for improvement. At the same time, the idea of teacher committees can cause eye-rolling because they seem like unproductive meetings where the same few teachers do all the work. Let's disband traditional teacher committees and instead create a group of teacher leaders whose primary purpose is to help all staff feel fulfilled and happy at work. Arthur C. Brooks, author of *Build the Life You Want* (written with Oprah Winfrey), teaches us what happiness really is: "The big driver of happiness is earned success: a person's belief that he has created value in his life or the life of others."[9] The team can start by creating a shared definition of teacher happiness at school and then ask all teachers to share celebrations and concerns regarding the school culture for staff. Then, they focus their work on the priority areas identified by their colleagues. After the teacher happiness committee is up and running, you can expand the idea to students by inviting student leaders to be part of a student happiness committee. Happiness for everyone is a foundation for success for everyone!

4. **Play and add something fun to your schedule every day.** If you are a secondary principal and like to make a fool of yourself trying to shoot hoops for a few minutes with the varsity basketball teams, go do that. If you are an elementary principal and you love pushing kindergarteners on the swings, go do that. Play fun music and dance with students. Whatever you need to do to remind yourself about the things you love the most about your job each day, be sure to schedule time to do it. When you are having fun, you are giving your teachers permission to have fun with students and with each other, and that increases happiness and job satisfaction. Students love to see you playful and laughing, and it builds relationships with them. Families love hearing from students that they love their principal. It is a win-win-win-win!

5. **Add a "Plus One" to all communication.** We communicate with stakeholders all the time, whether it is a quick email, a voicemail message, or a reminder on a messaging platform. One way to constantly build relationships is to always add a "Plus One" to that communication. Add a quick positive story or a reminder about how incredible your students are. You can even add a line about how much you enjoy your job. When people called my desk phone and got my voicemail, the first thing they heard was, "You have reached the desk of Allyson Apsey, the luckiest principal in the world." Start small and build a practice of pausing before you press Send on an email to consider how you can add a "Plus One" to build relationships.

A great principal forms great relationships with staff, with students, and with families. One of the key components of a great principal that's consistently identified is visibility. Students need to know who their principal is, not just in name but in daily interactions. They need to know they are important to the principal because it will make school and learning more important to them. Staff watches their leader like a hawk, and when it is clear that relationships with students are foundational to their principal, they become even more important to teachers.

> **Staff watches their leader like a hawk, and when it is clear that relationships with students are foundational to their principal, they become even more important to teachers.**

Family members are listening to the perceptions of the principal that students bring home, and it affects their own perception of the principal and the school as a whole. Building relationships with students is the easy work—they need your ear when they have a story, they need your heart when they have a problem, and they need your hand when they need help. Having that same patience with adults can be a bit more challenging but is just as necessary.

Besides George's wit and my wisdom (ha-ha), the best part of this book is the stories told by the contributing authors. We cannot think of a better way to begin the contributing author portion of the book than with the perspective of a student, so the next chapter features the voice of Taylor Teamann, who shares the power of a principal who focuses on building relationships with students. Get your tissues out because her story definitely made me tear up.

3 QUESTIONS FOR CONVERSATION AND REFLECTION

1 How might you demonstrate that everyone is valued and seen in your school? Who might feel unseen, and how can that be corrected?

2   What idea did you connect most with in this chapter, and how might you implement it in your school?

3   When reading this chapter, what was a source of pride? Something you already do to build relationships that is worthy of celebration?

CHAPTER 2

AHMO

BY TAYLOR TEAMANN

A leader is one who knows the way, goes the way, and shows the way.

—JOHN MAXWELL

This book is about what makes a principal great. The definition of great may vary from person to person, but you'd be hard-pressed to find anyone from Wylie ISD in Wylie, Texas, who doesn't think that Virdie Montgomery, my Wylie High School principal, is pretty darn great. I graduated just a few years ago, so I still remember what it feels like to be a student like it was yesterday. Sometimes, I still feel like a student. I had many amazing teachers and principals growing up, but Mr. Montgomery was different. He set the bar for relationships, commitment, and what it meant to be a part of something bigger than you are.

Some would say I didn't attend an ordinary high school. We took school pride seriously because Mr. Montgomery took school pride seriously. He drove a maroon car with a custom *AHMO* license plate, had numerous ties printed with the school logo, and even had a full-on school spirit suit set. He dedicated his entire life to being our school's leader, and I could not imagine it any other way. My high school wasn't like most. I might be a little biased, but I think Wylie High School is one of the best in Texas. "AHMO" is a slogan everyone in our part of town knows. It came from an old high school coach who used to shout and mumble. He would shout at his football players, and it would always come out sounding like "AHMO," as in "AHMO make you champions!" We chanted and yelled "AHMO" after everything. It was on our shirts and our cars, in our school cheers—it was everywhere. Growing up, people always asked me what it meant, and I never really had an answer for it. But now I know. I have realized that Virdie Montgomery *is* AHMO. He embodies everything those four letters stand for. AHMO means to stand out and make an impact. It means to be the best possible version of yourself in any and all situations, and to always lead with your best foot forward. Every student, teacher, and staff member knew that AHMO was more than a nonsense word. It was what made us a family. We had to wear our school spirit with pride. It didn't make sense to walk around in maroon and white if you didn't truly love our school, and everyone did.

My high school principal was someone who dedicated his entire life to leading and being the best possible principal he could be at all times. Virdie Montgomery was nothing short of impactful. He had a way of forming a personal connection with every single student who walked through the door and grew and maintained relationships for years past graduation. He would know things like our parents' names, what sports team we were on, what clubs we were interested in. There was no detail spared when it came to Virdie Montgomery. He hand-wrote letters to us all to celebrate our successes, and I've saved letters that he sent from all four years I was at Wylie High. How he had time to write, with as many students as he served . . . a real-life superhero! Having a relationship with every single person, especially in a school as big as ours, was no easy task. It has been a few years since I graduated, yet I always get a "Happy Birthday" shout-out every year on Facebook from him, as do many other students. He always made it a point to call you by your name, further demonstrating that he saw us as individuals. What I will always remember the most was that he was always present. He was out and about in the mornings, he came to *all* the sporting events, he was at every event, pep rally, game, match—you name it. His day started hours before school began and lasted well into the night. It was a priority of his to show up for all Pirate events. By him just being there, we as students knew that our principal was going to be present for us no matter what.

Each year we would have a school-wide competition. Each class had to get as many points as they could in different categories. We called this the AHMO game. One of the categories was to spot the principal out and about, and if we saw him or his car, we had to take a photo of it and tag him on social media. It was one of our favorite traditions, and finding Mr. Montgomery out on the town was always the category with the most points. He just had this way of being anywhere you needed him to be without you asking. The best part of all this was that Mr. Montgomery *loved* this just as much as we did! Every day he would update us about who was winning and was always so joyous when we would send him a picture we'd taken when spotting him. He reposted every picture we took every year. I'm sure his camera roll is still filled with them.

My favorite story to tell people about Mr. Montgomery is the "Elf on the Shelf" story. Each year for Christmas, he would dress up in a head-to-toe elf costume. He would then move and hide around the school all day, and it was our goal to spot the "Principal on the Shelf." Our favorite spot to see him in was atop the marquee sign in the front of the school. He would just sit there for a few hours waving at all the cars and talking to students, and even did an interview with a news station from there. To top it off, *Good Morning America* interviewed him, and it started a trend of educators all over dressing up and sitting in fun places. It was all anyone ever talked about during school around the holidays. Mr. Montgomery was the kind of principal who always surprised you. One day it might be an elf costume, one day it might be a pirate costume—we never knew what we were going to get. This was such a silly thing he did, but we loved it. The school morale was always so high, and we were able to see our principal just being silly and fun. Being a principal, especially a high school principal, is no easy task. They have to be an authority figure but still be someone everyone can lean on. One of my favorite things about Mr. Montgomery was that he acted and treated us like real people, not just kids. He was not afraid to dress up for the dress-up days, chant our silly chants, and just have fun with us.

> One of my favorite things about Mr. Montgomery was that he acted and treated us like real people, not just kids.

Our school was a tight-knit community. I had over six hundred kids in my class, and each class grew after that. We did everything as one. We celebrated every win, shook our heads at every loss, and felt everything together. The year I graduated also happened to be the year the world shut down. It may seem silly now, but at the time my class was devastated. No prom, no senior breakfast—none of the traditions we'd been waiting for. Once we knew we weren't going to be able to go back and finish our year, Mr. Montgomery did something . . . incredible. He and his wife, Pam, went on a Pirate adventure. He visited every single high school senior at their homes and gave them a note that said, *One day we'll look back on this and snicker* with a mini Snickers candy bar. It took weeks, but he got it done. This story also made it to *Good Morning America*, and Mars was so impressed they sent hundreds of candy bars for our graduating class.

Everything had already been so up in the air with what we were going to do or if we were going to be able to go back to school before we graduated. Our biggest concern was if we were going to get an actual in-person graduation ceremony and if Mr. Montgomery was going to be speaking. Thankfully, we got both. It was incredible not only to graduate but to have Mr. Montgomery be the one who dismissed us for the last time. At every ceremony he does, he ends by saying, "Class of (graduation year), you are dismissed," and all the students throw streamers and their hats in the air. The whole school talks about this moment from the very first day of ninth grade. Those words were so iconic and taken so seriously, we all could feel the power in that moment. It was so special to be a part of the last class that got to hear those words from him. Mr. Montgomery retired after our ceremony, but his impact on my life will never be forgotten.

3 QUESTIONS FOR CONVERSATION AND REFLECTION

1 Taylor said that Mr. Montgomery *was* "AHMO." As a principal, how would you like your students to define you?

2 Creating school pride is an important part of relationship building. What lessons will you take away from Taylor's story?

3 Mr. Montgomery lives out the idea of "go big or go home." What crazy, innovative idea are you dreaming about? What is your first step in making the idea a reality?

CHAPTER 3

Authentic Self and Relational Leadership

BY DR. MARCUS BELIN

Do not follow where the path may lead. Go instead where there is no path and leave a trail.

—RALPH WALDO EMERSON

When I assumed the role of principal, I was met with a stark reality—there was no comprehensive manual or blueprint for effective leadership in this position. The guidance I did receive fell short of addressing the multifaceted aspects of the role. Navigating a massive high school with around three thousand students was an initial challenge, and the journey ahead was entirely uncharted. The school's culture, environment, challenges, and surprises were unprecedented. How was I going to build authentic, positive, and powerful relationships with that number of students and staff members?

Amid this uncertainty, I found solace in embracing authenticity. Being my authentic self became the mission and the focus as I entered the building on my first day of work. I realized that being an authentic leader didn't necessitate acquiring a plethora of new skills; it demanded an unwavering commitment to being true to myself. While some might view this as cliché or foundational, it underscores the essence of leadership. Authenticity not only offers a sense of direction but also helps prioritize what truly matters when stepping into a leadership role. In essence, it's not about acquiring more knowledge but about staying true to oneself and being genuine in leadership endeavors.

Being an authentic leader means leading with honest and sincere intentions while maintaining a high level of integrity. Authentic leaders are self-aware, transparent, and open to vulnerability. They have a deep understanding of their values, beliefs, strengths, and limitations, and they use this knowledge to guide their actions and decisions. Trust can be formed quickly when leaders are authentic, and trust is at the core of relationship building.

> **Being an authentic leader means leading with honest and sincere intentions while maintaining a high level of integrity.**

In my journey as a building leader, I've garnered invaluable lessons over the past few years. These lessons serve as the bedrock for my personal growth and enhance my grasp of what truly constitutes an exceptional principal. While my learning journey is far from over, I'd like to highlight one particularly impactful lesson that offers profound insights into the essence of great principalship. This lesson provides a lens through which we can gain a deeper understanding of the qualities and attributes that distinguish remarkable school leaders.

Be Your Authentic Self

It took me a little time to grasp what it meant to be the building leader. I knew what I'd signed up for, but there always seemed to be an unspoken mold I felt I needed to conform to in order to truly inhabit the role. It involved my attire, interactions, the way I presented myself in meetings, and the decisions I made. In those initial months, I dedicated considerable energy to making the right first impressions, especially since there were faculty members with more experience than me. However, I soon realized that it wasn't about others' perceptions; people would form judgments regardless of my focus on those details. So, I put on my Jordan 1s, dressed comfortably in slacks and a polo, and confidently walked into my first faculty meeting of the school year. This was the authentic me, comfortable and poised as I shared my vision and expectations with the staff.

You see, authentic leaders inspire trust and loyalty by being consistent and reliable in their own shoes. They prioritize building genuine connections with their followers and foster an environment of mutual respect and collaboration. They communicate openly and honestly, sharing both successes and failures. Authentic leaders encourage diverse perspectives and actively listen to their team members, valuing their input and ideas. There is no cookie-cutter look to this role. Everyone who holds the title looks at this role differently and treats it differently. At the end of the day, we work for kids, and if we show up as our authentic selves, we can challenge the status quo of what it means to be the leader and what it means to be a change agent in the lives of the students and staff we serve.

The unexpected reality surrounding my appearance resonated with many students. Those Jordan sneakers I sported on countless days became instant conversation starters, bridging the gap and revealing my sincere interest in the students' success. It's simply who I am. As time passed, I took it a step further by not only lacing up Jordans but also zipping around the school on a hoverboard. This unconventional approach shattered preconceived notions. Students realized it wasn't about titles or roles; it was about my unwavering commitment to crafting the best experience for them.

I wanted my staff to understand it's okay to enjoy their work, to see education as a joyful journey, not a joyless task. This played a significant role in shaping our school's culture. Every day, I remind students that the worst two words in the English language are *if only*. It's about seizing opportunities, embracing authenticity, and making education a remarkable adventure of discovery.

Being a fifth-generation educator, I knew from an early age that education was my destined path. However, what truly mattered to me was not just the career itself but the kind of person and leader I aspired to be. I was determined to define the role I wanted to play in the lives of students and the school community I would serve. It wasn't about the title, but the values, the impact, and the relationships that I could foster to create a positive and enriching educational experience for both students and staff. This commitment to character and leadership has been my guiding light in this remarkable journey, reinforcing that being an educator is not merely a profession but a lifelong vocation that shapes futures and nurtures potential.

Growing up, I was fortunate to have remarkable role models who taught me invaluable life lessons. As I embarked on the journey of becoming a building principal, I delved into literature and curated a collection of quotes from my undergraduate and master's programs. My focus was clear: I wanted to define my leadership style, and at its core was the commitment to building meaningful relationships.

Throughout my life, relationships have been a driving force. These connections, forged over time, were instrumental in my personal and professional growth. They instilled in me a simple yet profound belief: as long as I treated people with respect and never gave them a reason not to trust me, I could reach great heights.

It's remarkable how this guiding principle has held true as I've progressed in my role. Building relationships with students, staff, and the broader school community has been not only personally rewarding but also instrumental in the success of our educational mission. These connections create trust, foster collaboration, and inspire a shared sense of purpose.

My journey as a building principal is a testament to the enduring power of these relationships. They have been the cornerstone of my leadership philosophy, reminding me daily that authenticity, respect, and trust form the bedrock of strong educational leadership. As I continue to grow and learn, I'm grateful for the wisdom imparted by my role models and the enduring impact of the relationships I've cherished along the way.

"We may have all come on different ships, but we're in the same boat now." These powerful words from Dr. Martin Luther King Jr. remind us that despite our diverse backgrounds, we share a common purpose in education: to create a nurturing and inclusive environment for students and staff.

Growth Points

1. **Live your values.** To be an authentic leader, start by reflecting on your core values. Then, actively live by them in your personal and professional life. Your actions should align with your principles, serving as a guiding light for your staff, students, and school community. This authenticity creates a culture of honesty and trust. It can also change the game of people's perception and make it a true and honest reality.

2. **Embrace vulnerability.** Being an authentic leader means recognizing your flaws and taking responsibility for your errors. When you show vulnerability, it nurtures an atmosphere of safety and openness where all members of the school community can feel comfortable doing the same. Embracing moments when you lack answers, question your own beliefs and gain insights from meetings significantly promotes a culture of acceptance among those observing your role. Some individuals mistakenly believe a principal should possess all the answers. However, if you do, you contradict the very essence of striving to be a lifelong learner.

3. **Continuously learn and adapt.** Authentic leaders are open to growth and change. Seek feedback from your students, staff, and parents. Their voices matter. Challenge the status quo, take calculated risks, and inspire your staff to embrace change as a means of growth and innovation, because kids deserve for their principal to be someone who continuously learns and adapts.

Denzel Washington once said, "At the end of the day, it's not about what you have or even what you've accomplished. It's about who you've lifted up, who you've made better. It's about what you've given back."[10] As school leaders, our role is not defined by titles or authority; it's about the relationships we build and the lives we impact. Authentic leadership is the key to making a difference in the lives of those we serve.

3 QUESTIONS FOR CONVERSATION AND REFLECTION

1   Dr. Belin started bringing his authentic self into his leadership when he started walking in his own shoes, quite literally. How might you bring your authentic self into your role as a current or prospective principal?

2   Which of Dr. Belin's three growth points do you most connect with and why?

3   How might you bring more joy into your work as a leader?

CHAPTER 4

Relationships Today, Results Tomorrow

BY KARI LACNY

All the knowledge in the world can't make a good leader: It's the care for the work and the people who collaborate with you that makes the difference, this is in large part because people want to follow a passionate leader. Someone who cares about not only the cause for which he or she is working, but also the other people who are involved in the effort. Passion for the projects, for the company and for the people involved are key to successful leadership.

—NOZOMI MORGAN

The success of any school depends on a leader being able to foster positive relationships at work. It is imperative employees feel seen, heard, and fulfilled in their work. But far too frequently, we neglect our relationships in favor of meeting work demands. Relationships in all areas need to be maintained with a certain degree of trust and interpersonal connection, and that takes time. Without a strong relationship with the person in charge, school employees will feel less comfortable asking for support during difficult situations and may begin to feel less job satisfaction over time.

Relationships and trust are foundational to learning, so it makes sense that one of the most important places strong relationships must be fostered is in an academic setting. A principal not only has to juggle demanding work-related tasks but must be an effective relationship builder with staff and students as well. I had the honor to work with one of the most amazing principals ever to grace a school. She will blush when I say this, but she is funny, empathetic, generous, and wickedly smart. She is a fabulous relationship builder and supportive principal, and she is just as gracious and understanding with students. You might be familiar with her name because it is on the cover of this book. I am excited to share with you that she practices what she preaches. Her name is Allyson Apsey. Not only was she my principal, she is an author and very sought after educational public speaker! Can you tell that I am proud of her?

I want to share my raw experience of Allyson as she guided me through overcoming the struggles I was facing. I use the word *raw* for a couple reasons—first, because my experiences with Allyson as my leader are raw and real, and mirror the experiences of my colleagues. I am writing this chapter, but honestly, any of my colleagues could be sharing the same message in their own words. The other reason I use the word *raw* is because that is how I felt when I met Allyson the first time. At the time, I had been teaching in my dream school district for eighteen years. A couple years before Allyson became my principal, in my sixteenth year of teaching, I was going through a difficult time as I transitioned out of a special education role that I adored into an unknown world of general education. I was leaving behind the familiar, and I was leaving behind a team that was incredibly supportive and fantastic to work with.

This story is about how Allyson's leadership helped me heal, so I won't expound on the negative other than to say that there were some challenges that first year teaching in general education that made me emotionally raw and very anxious about the transition. I was filled with self-doubt in a way I had never been as a teacher. But there was a ray of hope. I kept hearing my coworkers express excitement about someone who'd applied for the principalship of our building. They were on pins and needles waiting to hear if she would accept the job! She did, and the joy was palpable. I know the impact a leader can have on a school, positive or negative, and I was thrilled to hear my colleagues' enthusiasm about our new principal.

Even with all the positive energy around Allyson, I felt apprehensive about having a new leader and did not want to make any mistakes. During our first conversations, Allyson recognized my hesitancy to open up and be vulnerable. I didn't want to ask questions, offer suggestions, or share advice. She took the time to get to know me, my family, and my strengths as a teacher. Over the next few months, under her care and leadership, I felt like my confidence as a teacher was beginning to return. She encouraged me often to share teaching strategies with others, and, to be frank, she helped me heal.

By the end of the first semester with Allyson as our leader, I was able to trust the magic of this "new" beginning as a general education teacher. As I look back at that time a decade or so later, I reflect on what Allyson did that made her such an effective principal. I have experienced many principals during my career, and some were more effective than others. But being a relationship builder isn't something that principals have to be born with; it is something they can develop. Let's uncover what Allyson did for me, in the hope that it helps other educational leaders support their teachers in the same way.

1. **Before she speaks, she listens.** It is funny, as I think back on our conversations, I remember Allyson usually made me stop in my tracks. After I approached her with a question, she would ask powerful reflective questions that would cause me to pause and think. She was the epitome of "seek to understand before seeking to be understood." Every time we chatted, I

did most of the talking, even though I came to her for guidance. Not only did she develop a stronger understanding of my strengths and areas for growth because of this approach, I developed a stronger understanding of my strengths and my next steps after our discussions.

2. **She follows through with what she says she will do.** Allyson sent us a quick email every Monday morning that typically contained just two things: her weekly video announcements (more on those later) and a staff check-in. The check-in was a Google form that had one question: "How are you feeling about the week ahead?" I could check a box next to an answer that best matched how I was feeling, or I could put a comment in the "other" section. Every single time I asked for help on the check-in, Allyson was in my classroom that day, often within the hour. This is just an example of how she always followed through and built trust and relationships through her actions. Her consistency spoke volumes about how important we were to her. The reason I am so excited to have the opportunity to contribute to this book is to share that she was the real deal. Practicing what you preach is important as a school leader because it contributes to a culture of trust. Allyson always matched her actions to her promises.

3. **She not only gives constructive feedback, she also gives positive feedback.** Often, teacher evaluations and observations feel like "gotcha" moments, when leaders enter the classroom looking for what you are doing wrong so they can tell you how to do it right. When Allyson first started coming into my classroom, which she did almost daily, I could barely speak because I was so nervous. It took a semester of notes with specific positive feedback, conversations about the strengths she was seeing, and her encouragement about my skills for me to finally loosen up and accept that she came into my classroom looking for the good first. She asked me how I

wanted to grow and learn, and then supported me with my next steps. If you open the cupboard door in my classroom, you will still see all of the notes that Allyson left for me throughout the years, posted as a daily reminder of my strengths.

4. **Allyson goes above and beyond to make sure mental health for staff is valued.** Teaching is never easy, and I won't pretend that effective principals can take all the challenges away. But teaching feels much more rewarding and doable when there is a culture of grace, appreciation, and support in the school. One of the incredible things Allyson did was give up her office on those crazy days—like Halloween and Field Day—to create a "Zen Zone" for staff members. It gave us an opportunity to get away from it all and have a healthy snack and some downtime. When space became available, Allyson made a permanent "Zen Zone" so we would always have a spot in the school where we could take care of ourselves. Beyond that, Allyson taught us how to take care of each other through conversations about how to work best as a team, how to support each other through crises, how to be vulnerable with each other, and how to acknowledge each other's strengths.

> **Teaching feels much more rewarding and doable when there is a culture of grace, appreciation, and support in the school.**

5. **Allyson built a school that felt like a community of all stakeholders: staff, students, families, and community.** We became the school we dreamed of together because we wrote our own story, and then we told our own story. Allyson led the

way by creating the weekly video announcements that were sometimes silly but always informative and culture building. She involved students and staff in the creation of the videos and always shared the message of who we were as a school community. The video announcements were shared with students on Mondays and then were emailed out to families and community members. They highlighted the learning taking place in the classrooms, the character of our students, and our community events.

The Nozomi Morgan quote at the beginning of this chapter describes Allyson's leadership perfectly—all the knowledge in the world doesn't matter unless the people you are leading know you care deeply for them as individuals. The passion leaders have for our work with students inspires others to have the same level of passion. Principals set the tone for the school through their actions, and aligning actions with relationship building will set schools up for success every time. It's not a chicken-or-egg question; it is the necessary foundation for student learning.

> **The passion leaders have for our work with students inspires others to have the same level of passion.**

3 QUESTIONS FOR CONVERSATION AND REFLECTION

1 When you think of teachers who are struggling with self-doubt at your school, what connections do you make to Kari's story in this chapter?

2 Who in your school could use a pick-me-up in the form of a handwritten note about a specific strength?

3 What is your next step in creating a school of your dreams and then telling your school's story?

PILLAR TWO
Continuous Learner

Principals are leaders of learning environments, and great principals recognize the importance of being a model of continuous learning. Not only do principals need to learn to improve their leadership skills, they need to learn with, for, and about students, staff, and the community they serve. Great principals are visible in their pursuit to learn and grow and share their journey; they lead learning in their schools by learning alongside stakeholders.

PREFACE
Learning by Example

BY GEORGE COUROS

What we model is what we get.

—JIMMY CASAS

I have never been a big fan of "learning norms" (also referred to as "educational norms") in staff professional learning opportunities. It sometimes feels like they are fake collaborative agreements put into place by someone else, and we pretend that we all agree to them. Allyson disagrees with me a bit on this, and I am sure in some schools they work wonderfully, but I have often felt like there was a fakeness to the process.

But if you asked me to do learning norms for any staff professional learning day, I would simply say: "All I ask of you today is to learn in a way that you would expect from your students."

That's it. That's the tweet. Or the X. Or whatever it is called when you are reading this book.

Can we do it? Can we uphold the standards as principals, administrators, teachers, and staff members to learn in a way that we can expect from our students?

But maybe we should be asking, "What does learning look like that we expect from our students?" And maybe, "How has that changed?" That would be a great conversation to have.

Leading Learning by Example

In probably my fifth year of teaching, I remember one principal who was an incredibly nice man but not necessarily the epitome of a learner at this point in his career. It was his very last year in education, as he had announced his retirement at the beginning of the school year. That spring, our entire staff attended our mandatory education conference, and I distinctly remember the Friday afternoon session, when three hours stood between us and starting our weekend.

We were about five minutes into the final speaker of the day when I watched our principal stand up in the front row and slowly walk out of the session. There were zero cares to be had at that moment. He was retiring, so what was anyone going to say?

Here's the kicker. About five of us on that same staff watched in amazement, basically counted down sixty seconds, and then walked out of the same session. If our principal didn't see it as beneficial, then why would we?

You have heard the phrase "leading by example," but in education, "learning by example" comes first. Relevancy is contingent on our own willingness to grow.

What I did as a teacher because of what I saw in my principal really set the tone, not only for that moment but for the rest of the year. I also know that I am not alone, as I see the difference in the staff culture in schools around the world and their investment in their own learning based on the leader's willingness to learn and model what they expect.

Once You Are Done Learning, You're Done Leading

In a moment that was similar but had a very different outcome, I was working with a group of principals and sharing with them some new ways of thinking about educational technology and how it could impact schools. There was one principal there who was nearing the end of his career, and he kept asking the question "Is this really necessary?" You could tell that he was partially joking but also serious in his questioning. It was an interesting exchange because as he argued with me about much of what I was sharing and we bantered back and forth, I felt a genuine connection to this man.

About two weeks later, I received an email from a staff member at that same school who let me know this principal had announced his retirement at an event the previous night. What I didn't anticipate was the reason for his sudden announcement: me.

He shared in a speech that he hadn't been planning on retiring this year, but after I came, he had felt a certain pressure to continue his own learning and he saw how necessary it was for him to grow as a leader. He also realized he just didn't want to anymore. So instead of sitting in the principal's chair for another year or two, he decided that it was time for him to go. He knew that if he was to lead, his own learning was imperative, and he could not ask others to do something he was no longer willing to do.

Talk about a teachable moment! There was obviously some comedy in his speech, but the lesson he wanted to share with others was that if you are going to be in the principal's chair, you need to model the learning you expect from those you serve. If you aren't willing to do that, it is time to go. It was more important for him to leave a bit too early rather than much too late.

Are You the Lead Learner of Your School?

There is a video newsletter of my friend and former principal Tony Sinanis surrounded by five students sharing updates from around the school. Before Tony introduces each student, he introduces himself as the "lead learner" of the school. I have shown this video to others so many times, and often what resonates is that the example Tony sets for his community and directly with those students is that no matter your role and where you are on the traditional hierarchy of your school, your willingness to learn is imperative to the work that you do.

The term *lead learner* is not implying that you are the foremost authority on all things learning within your school, but it makes it clear that as a leader, your learning must be continuous if you want to be effective in your role.

The organizations that become the most irrelevant are often the ones that believe they are already "there" and have nowhere else to go. You might even refer to them as the "Blockbuster principals"; they have achieved a certain level of success and now will let the world move forward while they stand still.

But the best schools and leaders are focused on their own growth and continuous learning. In a shareholder letter from Amazon founder Jeff Bezos, he shared his company's focus on being continuously on "Day 1." He said that "Day 2" is stasis. Followed by irrelevance. Followed by an excruciating, painful decline. Followed by death. And that is why it is always Day 1. Say what you will about Amazon, but they are continuously trying to improve what they do to stay relevant. That takes a focus on continuous learning.

3 Types of Learning

As you read this or other books or partake in professional learning opportunities, you may notice they are often focused on leadership development and evolving pedagogies. These topics are very important, but we shouldn't be limited to those areas.

In my book *Innovate Inside the Box*, I focus on three types of learning that are essential for teachers: learning *for* your students, learning *about* your students, and learning *with* your students.

We are wonderful at the first, getting better at the second, and need to continuously develop on the third.

For principals, a simple tweak in the wording is necessary: learning *for* your community, learning *about* your community, and learning *with* your community.

You are doing the first by simply reading this book. As you read on, think about how you can improve on the second and the third fronts. How do we better learn about the people we serve, and how do we tap into their knowledge, wisdom, and experience to make our entire school community better? No matter how intelligent you are as an individual, you will never be as smart as your community as a whole. As the famous TV scientist Bill Nye shares, "Everyone you will ever meet knows something you don't." Definitely a true statement, but it doesn't matter much if you don't tap into that learning.

Moving Forward

There are areas in which you excel and areas in which you need to grow. That is true with every human on the planet.

As you continue to read this book, consider how you can make your learning visible. We often ask our staff and students to do something that they do not *see* us doing ourselves. Not that we aren't, they just don't see it. People are more likely to take steps forward on a path if they see footprints from others on the ground.

> **People are more likely to take steps forward on a path if they see footprints from others on the ground.**

Has something resonated with you in this book that can help your staff? Share it.

Have you struggled with a concept that you can improve in your own leadership? Share it.

As Tony shared in his video, being the lead learner is essential, but it doesn't mean that you have all the answers. It just means you have a willingness to look for them from different sources, other people, and within yourself.

One quality people often say that they love in their principal is that they never pretend they have all the answers, but they are always willing to learn so that they can help all of us and themselves get better.

As my good friend and superintendent Deidre Roemer shares, "Do new things, try new things. Be part of growing into the next version of what we need for kids."

That is the goal.

CHAPTER 5

Continuous Learner

BY ALLYSON APSEY

Success is a journey, not a destination. The doing is often more important than the outcome.

—ARTHUR ASHE

Here is another hard truth: principals are not hired because they know it all already. In fact, even after nineteen years in the principalship, I had learned just a fraction of what it takes to effectively run a school. It was my responsibility to seek out learning opportunities from school leader exemplars to expand my leadership skills. Additionally, it is a principal's responsibility to learn alongside teachers—not just to be physically there when professional learning is taking place, but to listen with curiosity and a desire to learn and grow. Put the phone away, close the laptop, ignore your smartwatch notifications, and engage in the learning norm that George taught us: learn in the same way you hope your students and teachers are learning. But if leaders are too busy to learn, what message does that send to staff, students, and the entire community about the importance of continuous learning and growth?

A principal as a continuous learner just makes sense. The primary role of school in a student's life is to promote learning, and everything we do to support the whole child and to meet the needs of every child is centered around creating an environment where learning can thrive. People look to the principal to see what is really important. When principals not only consistently invest in their own learning but also make their learning visible to their community, the message is clear: at this school, we are a community of learners, and that starts at the top.

> At this school, we are a community of learners, and that starts at the top.

A 2021 Wallace Foundation study, "How Principals Affect Schools and Students," points us in this same direction. Two of the four categories of leadership behaviors that positively impact school outcomes are linked to the idea that learning has to start with the principal. First, they found that effective principals engage in instructionally focused interactions with teachers, learning and growing their pedagogy skill base right alongside teachers. Second, the study found that successful principals focus on Professional Learning Community (PLC) collaboration with teachers, where the whole purpose is using evidence of student learning and the collective knowledge of educators to figure out how to create meaningful learning experiences for students.[11]

Do I ever wish I knew this when I was an early career principal! I was one of those new principals who mistakenly thought I got the job because I was smart and had all the answers. I thought I knew how to lead a school, or at least that I *should* know how to lead a school. Even when I had no clue what to do, I hesitated to ask for help because I thought I might be found out as an imposter. I don't know if I have ever been more wrong. Great leaders know that they don't have all the answers, and they are always looking for ways to learn and grow. Great leaders focus on asking skillful questions, and they are constantly researching to gather new ideas and information. Great leaders hear about something amazing happening in another school or district and rather than sadly thinking, "Dang, I wish I thought of that," they excitedly think, "That's awesome! Good for them. How can we make that happen at our school?"

I am going to age myself here, but I became a principal before Facebook and Twitter even existed. It was more challenging back in those pre–social media times to get connected to inspiring principals around the country. In those first years of the principalship, I distinctly remember being faced with challenges and then heading to my office to rack my brain for ideas. I was so mad at myself when I could not come up with brilliant solutions on my own. Or worse, I would come up with a plan to solve the problem and then implement it without getting feedback or input from teachers, and then was shocked when it failed miserably. Today's effective principals are connected to other effective principals because they want to learn from the incredible things other leaders are doing. Today's effective principals involve teachers and other staff in decisions because they know that input from those who will implement the decision is crucial for success.

Moving from Reactionary to Proactionary

I was much wiser when I started my second principalship and entered that role with eleven years of leadership experience under my belt. My experience mainly taught me that I still had a lot to learn, and it taught me to be humble and confident enough to ask for help, input, and feedback. I was replacing a beloved and effective principal, and one of the best things I did was befriend her and look to her for guidance. It helped smooth the transition because the staff knew I was seeking out her input and that I trusted the leader they loved so much. It helped them trust me, knowing that I was open to learning from and being coached by the former principal rather than threatened by her.

We all need a coach, even the most seasoned school principals. Leadership coaching is an opportunity to get real-time feedback, which is sorely missing for most principals. The adage "No news is good news" does not apply here. No news means no feedback, which means no growth.

The COVID-19 pandemic truly wreaked havoc on the idea of a principal as a leader of learning, and I experienced this firsthand. Before the pandemic, I prided myself in having a standing desk on wheels and spending my days as a principal out in the hallways, in classrooms, in the cafeteria, and out on the playground. I would eat my lunch while standing in our rotunda, the heart of the school, feeling guilty as droplets of juice fell on the tiled floor as I peeled my orange. (I cleaned it up, don't worry!)

Before the pandemic, I didn't have a chair at my desk in my office because when I was in there, I didn't want to get comfortable. I knew that when I was *not* in my office, I was always in the right place at the right time. A leader cannot possibly know what teachers and students need unless she is out among them the majority of the day. Leading up to all the changes the pandemic brought, I felt like I was on my way to aligning my day-to-day leadership behaviors to the needs of the school community. The scales were beginning to tip toward spending more time learning and proactively planning and a little less time being reactive. Rather than running around putting out fires, systems were in place so I was able to have deep conversations with teachers about pedagogy, evidence of student learning, and their goals.

And all that flew out the window in March of 2020. We had mandatory new school leadership tools; rather than wearing my fanny pack with speakers around, I needed to wear a tool belt to hold my tape measure. My desk on wheels gathered spider webs because I was tethered to the office as we navigated ever-changing orders from the health department, upset and confused parents, quarantine phone calls, student illnesses, staff communication, and so much more. As the school leader, I felt like I needed to overhear all the conversations to clarify the information, answer questions, and calm the rising tension.

All my school leader friends are nodding along here and reflecting on their own return-to-school circumstances. It felt like all of the leadership progress we had made slammed into a brick wall and we became "survival principals," doing what we had to do to stay in school. Our jobs shifted into 100 percent reactive mode, and we definitely were running around like chickens with our heads cut off. But here's the thing. As I work with principals across the country, we are often still running around playing Whac-A-Mole with problems. It's almost a muscle-memory problem. We have trained ourselves to constantly look at our phones, our email, listen to the walkie-talkie. It's reflexive to grab for one of those devices every few seconds.

I am starting to see principals put the devices away and create sacred time to begin to align their daily behaviors to leadership best practices. This is hard work because it means looking closely at what they can take off their plates, and what they need to prioritize. Principals need to be constantly learning about the needs of their school community, developing their own skills as leaders, and then do the most important part—turn their learning into an action plan to support the continuous improvement of student learning.

What can principals do to be continuous learners? Here are five quick, simple tips:

1. **Choose five inspiring leaders to follow closely on social media.** They don't need to be in the education field to provide valuable learning. Spend twenty minutes once or twice a week scrolling through their feeds to learn alongside them. They say you are who you surround yourself with, so use social media for good to become a stronger leader through learning from leaders you admire.

2. **Spend ten minutes a day reading nonfiction books about education or leadership, or listen to a podcast that supports**

your learning. When we learn in small, bite-sized chunks, we give ourselves time to process the learning and connect it to our own work.

3. **Share your learning.** As learning becomes a part of your regular routine, you will find opportunities to share your learning with staff, students, and families. Not only will they benefit from the learning you share, they will see you as a continuous learner and a wonderful role model.

4. **Learn alongside teachers every chance you get.** Working hard side by side is the best way to build relationships. Not only that, learning alongside teachers will help principals understand the challenges they are facing in the classroom, and the successes they are experiencing.

5. **Conduct "stay interviews."** Rather than wait until staff members leave to learn about the challenges they face at the school, conduct interviews with current staff members to learn about why they stay at the school and how things could be better for them. This valuable learning will help principals know what to keep, what to modify, and what to fix.

We are in the business of learning, and great principals must be continuous learners. We cannot say that we don't have time to learn when one of the most important attributes of a great principal is seeking out new learning and sharing it. As George pointed out, learning about your community, for your community, and how to best lead your community is a top priority for effective school leaders. Not only does it model the importance of continuous improvement, but it demonstrates a humble heart and putting ego aside.

3 QUESTIONS FOR CONVERSATION AND REFLECTION

1. What percentage of your day do you spend in proactive versus reactive mode? How might you shift that balance to spend just 10 percent more time in proactive mode?

2. Which of the five tips shared in this chapter will you adopt or modify and put into practice right away?

3. What did you learn recently, and how can you share it with teachers and/or students to model the importance of being a continuous learner?

CHAPTER 6

Learning Out Loud: Turning Up the Volume on Student Voices

BY DR. MARY HEMPHILL

That is what learning is. You suddenly understand something you've understood all your life, but in a new way.

—DORIS LESSING

In the world of education, where no two years are alike, school leaders take on a role that has the power to influence the entire learning community, and that role is the lead learner.

At the heart of any learning community is a leader who "learns out loud." The role of the lead learner sets the tone for a culture of continuous learning by inspiring both educators and students to embark on and embrace their own learning journeys. While it is not always a highly regarded or popular role, someone has to model the way forward. Someone has to grapple with the questions, make new meaning from old information, and articulate the process along the way for others to observe.

This responsibility requires the leader to commit to the process of uncovering new knowledge, staying curious and adaptable to new ideas, and ultimately fostering an environment where everyone is encouraged to learn, evolve, and reach their full potential. Sometimes, the lead learner comes face-to-face with information that causes them to recalibrate and reassess everything.

I was in my fourth year as a principal when my role as lead learner changed my journey forever.

I had been the principal of our elementary school for almost two years, and our school community was transforming for the better. When I was appointed principal, our school had just received a failing report card from the state department of education; assessment scores were dismal with a morale to match. Our leadership team had a heavy lift ahead of us, but we were committed to positive change. At the beginning of our journey, we knew that to create a catalyst for change we would need to hear the voices of leaders at every level. We decided to start with our most important stakeholders—our students—and it was then that we developed the One-Minute Meeting.

What if we spent one minute with every student in the building and asked them three specific questions about their learning journey in our school?

- Question 1: How are you today?
- Question 2: What is your greatest celebration, or what are you most proud of from the past nine weeks?
- Question 3: What challenges or concerns are you experiencing in your class(es) or in our school from the past nine weeks?

For almost two years, our students met with me and our assistant principal once a quarter and engaged in the One-Minute Meeting, sharing their realities, their experiences, their celebrations, and their challenges. For two years, our school community listened, leaned in, and leveraged their answers to help us build a deeper understanding of their lives, how they learned best, and what mattered to them as learners in our community. Our students informed our pedagogy, our instructional practice, and even our policies for shared decision-making. And that first year we moved our school from an F on the state report card to a D.

We were weeks away from the state assessments in year 2, and I decided to begin my first set of One-Minute Meetings in the third-grade hall. As I wheeled my large principal chair and cart toward Mrs. Parker's classroom door, I could hear the buzz of learning from the hallway. Our students were familiar with the process at this point in the year, and when I popped my head in, Mariah eagerly made eye contact with her teacher and bounced toward the door. I quickly grabbed a student chair from the kidney table and joined her in the hall.

Mariah made herself comfortable in the cushy office chair, and I assumed the position in the student chair with my laptop on my knees, ready to capture her responses.

"How are you today?" I asked.

"I am doing amazing, Dr. Hemphill. I had a blueberry muffin for breakfast, and I passed my math exam with a B!" she responded with light in her eyes.

"That's amazing! I love blueberry muffins, too, and I know you had a goal for passing your math exam, and I'm proud of you for reaching it. What is your greatest celebration, or what are you most proud of from these past nine weeks?"

Mariah paused. Then she clapped her hands together and said, "Dr. Hemphill, my sister just exited her EC classes, and we are going to be in the same reading group for the first time since kindergarten!"

Now it was my turn to pause. Mariah was referring to her twin sister, Milan, who had indeed just exited the exceptional children's program weeks before. This particular program required that Milan engage in specialized Tier 2 instruction in English Language Arts based on her individualized education plan (IEP) goals in the area of reading. At this moment, however, Mariah was not celebrating instructional mastery, the newest teaching practice in our classrooms, or a policy we developed. She was celebrating a core memory that she would get to experience with her wombmate for the first time in years—reading in small groups.

Mariah's perspective was so powerful because it shifted the focus from academic achievements and educational policies to the emotional connection between her and her twin sister, Milan. While others may have been caught up in celebrating instructional mastery or the implementation of new teaching practices, Mariah recognized the significance of a core memory that she and Milan would get to share for the first time in years. Her authentic perspective highlights the importance of personal connections, experiences, and the joy that can be found in simple, meaningful interactions, reminding me and our school community that education is not solely about academic success but also about fostering relationships and creating lasting memories on the journey.

It was then that the principal became the student. That day Mariah showed me a new way to create positive transformation in our school—through students' lived experiences. Prior to that moment, I had been focusing on the "what" of school transformation. I poured into the processes, the pedagogy, and the practice, working to ensure leaders at every level understood the protocols that led to change. I had not been as focused on the "who" of school transformation. Our students' lived experiences fueled the way they experienced teaching and learning in our school, and my job as the continuous learner was to take their experiences and translate them into valuable lessons for our school community.

> **Our students' lived experiences fueled the way they experienced teaching and learning in our school.**

Mariah's celebration of a shared experience with her sister in the same reading group unlocked a new perspective that eventually helped me guide our teachers, support staff, and community stakeholders to focus intensely on creating quality experiences for our students. Once I shared this encounter with our leadership team and school improvement team, we embarked on some critical shifts in our building:

- **Embedded the Feelings Wheel into all core content areas** to allow our students access and exposure to language that helps them more accurately express their thoughts and experiences through spoken and written language. The Feelings Wheel is an interactive infographic that helps to recognize and understand one's emotions by starting with seven of the big emotions we learn first as humans—sad, happy, surprised, bad, fearful, angry, disgusted—and find deeper, more contextual words and phrases to express those feelings through spoken or written language. Visit FeelingsWheel.com to see it.

- **Introduced journaling into the morning and afternoon routines** as a starter or exit ticket activity for students to capture their experiences. Students were invited to share their journal reflections only if they felt safe and comfortable enough to do so.

- **Began the Friday Huddle across grade levels,** which allowed students and their teachers to huddle up on Friday afternoons before wrapping up the week to celebrate personal and learning milestones, achieved goals, new discoveries, or significant experiences as a collective unit, and end the week on a positive note.

As Mariah answered that question during her One-Minute Meeting, her voice filled with pride and expectancy, and I couldn't help but be moved by her story. Her celebration of her twin sister was a testament to the power of perseverance and the transformative impact of celebrating growth. Through that encounter, which lasted only sixty seconds, I realized that by acknowledging and celebrating the achievements, no matter how small, we can inspire students to believe in their own potential.

Sometimes the journey of continuous learning means you have to see the answer through fresh eyes. Mariah's insight helped us move our school from a D rating to a B over the course of the next year, and it only took a minute to learn that our students' experiences are all we need to create the positive change we had been searching for.

Key Strategies to Embrace Continuous Learning:

1. **Empower student voice in decision-making.** To truly transform the educational experience, school leaders must actively involve students in the decision-making process. By creating platforms for student voice, such as student councils, advisory boards, or regular feedback sessions, leaders empower students to contribute their perspectives, ideas, and aspirations. This not only fosters a sense of ownership and engagement but also ensures that decisions are made with a deep understanding of student needs and aspirations.

2. **Foster a culture of reflection and collaboration.** To promote continuous learning, school leaders can establish a culture of feedback and reflection. Encourage regular feedback loops among educators, where they can provide constructive input to one another and engage in reflective practices. Additionally, create platforms for self-reflection, such as journaling or peer coaching, to encourage educators to critically examine their teaching practices and identify areas for improvement. By fostering a culture of feedback and reflection, school leaders create an environment that values continuous growth and encourages ongoing learning.

3. **Establish a culture of celebrations.** To reinforce the importance of growth and achievements, establish a culture of celebrations within the school community. This involves creating regular opportunities to recognize and celebrate the successes, milestones, and efforts of both students and

69

educators. Implement initiatives such as monthly or quarterly celebrations, where outstanding achievements, progress, and contributions are acknowledged publicly and authentically. Additionally, encourage the sharing of success stories and accomplishments through newsletters, internal digital apps, social media platforms, or dedicated bulletin boards. By elevating celebrations, school leaders foster a positive and supportive environment that motivates and inspires continuous learning and growth.

3 QUESTIONS FOR CONVERSATION AND REFLECTION

1   What connection did you make to Dr. Hemphill's One-Minute Meetings, and what is your first action step based on your connection?

2   How might understanding students' lived experiences accelerate student learning in your school?

3   What idea shared in this chapter will you adopt or modify? How will you hold yourself accountable for making it happen?

CHAPTER 7

Take a Breath, Close Your Eyes, and Go for It

BY CJ REYNOLDS

Your life needs a few hold your nose and jump moments.

—JEFF FOXWORTHY

You could hear the bass pumping from the speakers in Room 106 all the way down the first floor hallway. I found out later that students from other classes were asking for hallway passes to the bathroom just so they could peek through my classroom window to catch a glimpse of what was going on. It got to the point that I had to lock the classroom door so that other students would stop coming into our already overfilled classroom.

I knew the special visitor to our classroom had the potential to get loud and incredibly excited, but this was more than I expected. In retrospect, I'm not sure how I thought having a DJ come to class to teach the art and science of mixing and scratching would not be loud and attract attention.

About ten minutes into class, a knock came to the door, but it was too loud to hear it. A moment later my principal, Dr. Noah Tennant, walked in after unlocking the door. I quickly walked over to him, feeling pretty certain that at best I was going to be told to shut this down and at worst we were going to have to have a meeting about what passed as an appropriate lesson in our school.

I addressed him immediately before he could say anything. "I'm so sorry this is so loud. I didn't think about that. But look at how excited and engaged the kids are. This is the most participation I've seen from some of these guys all year." To my utter surprise, the first words he said were "This is awesome!" He explained that had heard our class all the way from his office and had come to see for himself what was going on. Dr. Tennant stood there with a huge smile on his face and watched the students perform for another ten minutes or so before leaving. As he closed the door behind him, the music happened to stop, and one of my students, Aquil, asked what everyone else was thinking.

"Reynolds, did you just get in trouble?"

"No," I said. "Dr. Tennant said this was awesome."

They looked as amazed as I did.

What Dr. Tennant saw in that moment was what my colleagues and their curious hallway-wandering students couldn't see. And the reason Dr. Tennant saw it was because he was a learner first—always. He came in expecting to see good things and to learn what was going on in my classroom that was causing so much excitement. He did not make assumptions or base his thinking on what others were saying; he wanted to learn for himself. A class had created a learning moment together in which every student was engaged. My students who had been writing, peer reviewing, editing, and rewriting poetry for weeks were stepping to the front of the classroom to pour out their hearts and souls against the beats being spun, nervously and with vulnerability. Every student, even the ones who were always late to class and slept most of the day, were on their feet, either waiting to try their hand at the turntables or to share a verse with their classmates.

Dr. Tennant and I began working in West Philadelphia in the same year. He was the new principal, and I was the new ninth-grade literature teacher. He was unlike any administrator I had ever worked for before. Most of the school leaders I had worked with before were more like administrators than leaders. Their jobs were to keep the status quo, put out small fires, and keep the school running. They were not interested in learning from their teachers. But Dr. Tennant was different. He was not there just to lead, he was there to learn. He was the first leader I had worked for.

The difference was instantly evident during our first back-to-school staff meeting that year. Dr. Tennant started the meeting as a lot of principals do. He reminded us that we were there to serve students and their families, to work together to create opportunities for our students to become who they were meant to be. And that he would be there to help us in any way we felt would help us meet these goals. Then he asked a question none of the staff had ever been asked: "So who has an idea on how we can do this?" Again, wanting to learn from us rather than tell us what to do.

I remember sitting there not sure if he was serious. Did he really expect us to share? We were used to being consumers rather than producers during staff meetings.

Tennant repeated, "Come on. Someone has an idea. What is it?"

A brave teacher then spoke up and suggested that the practice of creating and submitting formalized lesson plans was a waste of teachers' time and energy. It was time that could be used helping students and doing what was needed to create engaging learning experiences for them. Without missing a beat, Dr. Tennant said, "I think you are right. Going forward, all teachers with three or more years of experience are no longer required to submit formal lesson plans."

Wait, what?!? We were stunned. No more formal lesson plans?! What happened next was a rush of suggestions from the entire staff about ways we could make our school a place that would make students and their teachers *want* to show up every day. Not every suggestion was adopted, but teachers were told yes more than no.

That next school year was a flurry of experimentation. Dr. Tennant had given us not only the gift of autonomy but the gift of being able to fail forward. He was a continuous learner, and he expected the same from us. Teachers began creating classes based around the math and science of video games, STEM projects with Lego, real-world entrepreneurship, and personal finance. We were creating classes, lessons, and learning experiences with *our* students in mind.

> Dr. Tennant had given us not only the gift of autonomy but the gift of being able to fail forward.

Each teacher who pitched an idea had to connect it to the curriculum and had regular observations and check-ins with administrators and their PLC. Some of these ideas were unsuccessful, and those teachers had to pivot, but Dr. Tennant constantly worked with us to find the lessons and not just focus on the losses.

I created a class called the History of Hip-Hop where I designed a curriculum that connected the English Common Core Standards to the four main tenets of hip-hop: DJing, MCing, graffiti art, and breakdancing.

I realized in that first marking period that my passion for and knowledge of hip-hop would not be enough to create the type of student-centered learning experience my students needed and wanted. So following Dr. Tennant's model of lessons over losses, I shifted how the class was structured. Instead of only reading, writing, and discussing the history of the elements of hip-hop, we began searching Philadelphia for community members who would be willing to help these lessons come alive. Graffiti artists built the connection between symbolism and street art. Entrepreneurs led close reading and listening workshops to help students annotate and interpret through the lens of albums like Jay-Z's *The Blueprint*. DJs like Cosmo Baker helped our Friday rap battles and poetry readings come alive, even if they were a little too loud.

Dr. Tennant created a culture among his staff that challenged us to go beyond identifying problems. He challenged us to learn together— to learn about our students, about each other's strengths, and even learn from our failures. He challenged us to think, craft, and offer solutions. Solutions may be imperfect and sometimes questionable (like bringing a graffiti artist to your classroom), but this freedom allowed teachers to think outside of the box for their students. We ended up creating learning experiences that resulted in increased student attendance, higher student engagement, decreased teacher turnover, and a noticeably reinvigorated excitement for teaching and learning among staff and students. He created the blueprint that allowed us to be an example to our students of what it looks like to try, fall short, readjust, and keep going.

The comedian Jeff Foxworthy says that "your life needs a few hold your nose and jump moments." Moments where you are not sure of the outcome but that offer such an incredible return on investment that you have to take a breath, close your eyes, and go for it.

3 QUESTIONS FOR CONVERSATION AND REFLECTION

1   In what way could you offer your staff the opportunity to not just identify but solve some of the challenges your school is facing?
2   How might you create a culture in which your staff are able to focus on lessons over losses?
3   What idea shared in this chapter will you adopt or modify? How will you hold yourself accountable for making it happen?

CHAPTER 8

Model
the Way

BY DR. EMILY KAY FREELAND

Leaders are more powerful role models when they learn than when they teach.

— ROSABETH MOSS KANTER

But you go first!" Words I repeatedly said while growing up. As the little sister, I frequently was challenged by my older sister. The setup was always something like, "I bet you won't," "I dare you to," or "You are too scared to," and I still hear myself saying, "I will if you will" and "If you go first." Maybe you had similar experiences growing up. Isn't it funny that as children and even as adults we find comfort in following the lead of a sibling, friend, or colleague when it comes to trying something we perceive as difficult?

After serving in the role of instruction and leadership coach for a few years, I found myself hearing that same expression, "You go first," while working one day with a school leadership team. I had been working with this school for two years, and we were entering our third year together. The focus of the principal had always been raising the levels of thinking and engagement with students. Our first year, we focused on questioning in the classroom. We then moved to academic discourse in the second year. His staff meetings and school-wide professional learning were always targeted to provide more strategies in these areas, and we were seeing growth in the teachers' practices, as well as in the student work products.

When we began planning for this third year, the principal shared that he'd attended a conference over the summer that included a session on microteaching. He was so enthusiastic as he talked about how the presenter made the process seem simple while also highlighting the huge impact it can have on teaching and learning. His excitement evoked a flurry of questions and ideas, and, in very short order, the team was mirroring his eagerness to make this the focus of the year.

As we began developing the plan for presenting this to the staff, one team member said to him, "You should go first." I vividly remember the expression on his face as he began to process that request. He went from surprised, to resistant, to amenable to the idea. As soon as the "go first" challenge was presented, the other team members began talking about the impact of having their leader model the way. We discussed the vulnerability required and the value of him sharing his entire experience from start to finish (video included), along with all of the accompanying emotions. What an impact it could have in getting the staff to feel safe as they took the risk and followed his lead!

As he and I debriefed at the end of that day, he shared with me how this idea of going first was pushing him way out of his comfort zone. He had not taught a lesson in a classroom in a long time. But he also shared that he knew the importance of doing the hard things he was asking his teachers to do. Instead of using flowery words of encouragement to get them to jump in, he knew his willingness to try microteaching a lesson himself would be more powerful. So, he did! And he shared his video in the next faculty meeting. He and the staff processed how he asked questions and the effectiveness of the discussion protocol he used. He also filled in the emotions he felt along the way and what

WHAT MAKES A GREAT PRINCIPAL

he wished he had done differently. He went on to share how much he had learned in the process, from planning to implementation. It was then that he asked his staff if they would be willing to try this as a strategy for improvement.

When I returned for my next visit, he was excited to tell me that all but one teacher had tried microteaching and recorded themselves. He also shared that many of his teachers told him they were only willing to try it themselves because he went first. The teachers said that it was his vulnerability and transparency that convinced them it was safe to take the risk. Over the course of the year, we saw classrooms transformed and teachers seeking feedback from their peers to improve their practices. And it all started with the challenge from his team and his willingness to "go first" and model the way.

> **The teachers said that it was his vulnerability and transparency that convinced them it was safe to take the risk.**

In my role as a coach, I frequently work with school leaders who value continuous learning and encourage their teachers to participate in professional learning opportunities. But too often, those leaders forget the value of participating in that learning themselves. Let's consider the actions of this principal in more detail. First, he chose to attend a summer conference to invest in his own learning. While there, he didn't just attend sessions that sounded interesting or had a catchy title. He sought out sessions that targeted the learning focus of his school and avoided sessions that might divert his attention from the goals his team had set. He also challenged himself to take in as much as he could each day. I know this because I was at that conference too. He found time at the close of the conference to debrief with me all he had gleaned. He prioritized what he might share with his team at their first meeting so they could determine the steps necessary to move forward with the work they had been doing.

Once he was back at school with his leadership team, he shared his learning and the ideas he had for implementation. But instead of pushing only his own thoughts forward, he asked his team for their ideas on how best to proceed. The team members looked for personal connections to the work they had done the previous year and also tried to think about how their peers might respond to these new ideas. They discussed group dynamics and additional learning needed. They collaborated around the logistics of tackling microteaching as a whole staff, from the time needed for learning and planning to the equipment needed for recording. Every attempt was made to remove barriers for success. Together, the team developed a schedule and a topic focus that drove the learning and practice for the year. Because this principal sought input and feedback from the team to develop action steps to address the goals for the year, we ended that meeting with an actionable plan that included time for teachers to have supported collaborative planning to prepare for their lesson, as well as to debrief their own learning.

It would have been very easy for this principal to find reasons and make excuses to avoid the microteaching lesson. Instead, he embraced the challenge and all he might learn in the process. Interestingly, he had been a middle school math teacher but chose to teach a reading lesson in third grade. He went beyond the challenge, way out of his comfort zone, to maximize the experience. When it came time to share his lesson experience, he thoughtfully walked through the steps he took to prepare and deliver his lesson. He described to the teachers how he read about and researched the strategies he wanted to use. He observed a reading lesson in another grade level and compared what he saw to the standards for that grade level as well as for third grade. As he began recounting his experience with the staff, he described how nervous he was and his fear that the lesson would not go well. He also talked about the relief he felt when it was over. As they viewed his video together, he and the staff identified parts of the lesson that went well and things that could have been different. They evaluated how he met the expectations for questioning and academic discourse. It was such an impressive display of vulnerability and transparency! Instead of finding someone else to take the lead, he stepped to the front and modeled the way.

As we began implementing the action steps outlined by the leadership team, the principal was present and participated in all learning sessions, including the supported planning sessions. He made sure it was clear that he was an active participant through the entire process. He knew it was important that he continue learning alongside the teachers and not check out once his microteaching lesson was over. As a result, collaboration among staff increased. They invited each other into their classrooms. They began lesson studies and continued to refine their classroom teaching practices. The collective learning on his staff was transformed, all because he was willing to go first.

3 QUESTIONS FOR CONVERSATION AND REFLECTION

1 How do you solicit input and feedback from your staff in creating professional learning goals for the school?
2 How do you model the way with vulnerability and transparency regarding your learning?
3 How might you ensure that you are an active participant in all aspects of your school's professional learning?

PILLAR THREE
Talent Cultivator

Effective principals understand that the collective wisdom of their staff is the school's greatest asset. They recognize the strengths in every staff member and support each team member in seeing their own strengths and identifying their next steps. Great principals not only shine a light on the talent among the staff, they create a culture where teachers recognize and celebrate each other's talents. Great principals know that when teachers feel supported, strong, and powerful, they feel equipped to work through any challenge.

PREFACE
Start from Strengths

BY GEORGE COUROS

Help others achieve their dreams and you will achieve yours.

—LES BROWN

In many educational circles, I am known as the "change" guy. My focus for years has been on how to help people embrace change and, more importantly, how to help them initiate it. The best way to deal with change is to create it yourself.

Because of this, I am often asked this question: "If you were to start over as a principal and go to a new school, what is the first thing you would change?"

My answer, no matter the school, the time, or the community, is always the same: "Nothing."

Too often, we want to push our own personality onto a new school community and not embrace any of the things that have been done in the past that are good. This is actually a move that politicians make and why many people are increasingly frustrated with governments around the world. A new person is elected and wants to undo everything that was done prior, because keeping it might be an admission that the last person did some things well. How can any community build momentum if we are always undoing, redoing, and newdoing (I just made that term up, but I have no idea how to make the trademark sign!) initiatives just so the new person in the position of leadership can be the one provided the credit?

Although there are some political aspects to the job of principal, principals are not politicians.

Maria Shi, the director of PayPal, knows how important it is to bring out the best in the people we serve. She eloquently states, "I measure my own success as a leader by how well the people who work for me succeed."

This doesn't happen by ignoring the past and replacing the new. It is about building on the current strengths of those already there.

Fixing or Valuing?

So if I were to enter a new building as principal and change nothing, what *would* I do?

This is going to seem a bit technical, but as I was getting to know everyone, I would create a spreadsheet and write every staff member's name down, and in a column to the right of their name, I would write, *What is this person's passion and/or strength?*

Until I can fill out that form in its entirety, and—this is really important—people *know* I know their strength and or passion, nothing changes in that school.

"But won't that take forever?"

It won't be quick.

Do you know what takes longer? Staff pushing back on every initiative and idea because they don't trust you, and they are wondering how long it will be before the next person comes in to take over the role.

This is such a necessary process because if people think you are there to "fix them," they will fight you on everything.

If people know they are valued and see that you are trying to bring out the best in them through what is already there, they will be much more willing to explore new ideas.

I shared this in *The Innovator's Mindset* and believe it to this day: "To create a culture where innovation flourishes, we have to realize that, in many cases, we already have everything we need; we just need to figure out how to tap into it."

You don't always have to rip down the old to build the new.

But you can't build the new on your own.

Have You Tried Asking Them?

So how do you cultivate talent through the passions and strengths of the people you serve? Well, sometimes all it takes is asking a question.

As a principal and assistant principal, every year I would send out an email to staff and ask a variation of this question: "If you could have your dream job within this school, what would it be?" It was amazing how many people would share that they wanted to do a totally different job than the one they were currently doing. I remember an incredible first-grade teacher, who seemed to love the role, sharing that she wanted desperately to teach middle school students. And when we had a retirement in the position, she was placed there before we had even considered posting the job.

What happens often is that we don't ask the question and instead give new staff the cable company "new customer" deal, where they get all the perks of signing up for new service, while ignoring the customers who have shown loyalty to their spotty internet for years. If you are willing to offer exciting opportunities to attract new talent, you better ensure that your current staff has some incentive to stay as well.

Could we always make the requested staffing switch? No, truthfully, we couldn't make the requests work all the time, but we were able to accommodate requests way more than we initially thought we could. But just asking the question mattered. One of the best responses I ever received to that question was a teacher saying, "I am actually doing my dream job right now, and I definitely don't want to do anything else. It does make a difference that you are asking, though, and I appreciate you taking the time."

Moving Forward

One of my philosophies as a teacher, administrator, and even as a dad is "How do we move people from *their* point A to *their* point B?"

I felt weird adding in "dad" to the sentence above, but as I thought about it, I realized how different my own kids are, what they are excited about, and how I help them grow. I don't expect them to react to the same things or become the same person. They are beautifully unique, just like everyone else.

But if we want to move people from *their* point A to *their* point B, it is necessary to know who they are, what they are passionate about, and how we bring out the best in them, which in turn, I hope, is the standard practice in our classrooms.

As Peter F. Drucker shared, "It takes far less energy to move from first-rate performance to excellence than it does to move from incompetence to mediocrity." Recognize the gifts you already have, whether it is your first or fifteenth year in the role (do principals last that long, other than Allyson?), and those gifts will be given back to you and your school community on repeat.

> **Want to cultivate talent? Start with what people are already good at. That is always your best bet.**

Want to cultivate talent? Start with what people are already good at. That is always your best bet.

85

CHAPTER 9

Talent Cultivator

BY ALLYSON APSEY

Leadership is not about being in charge. It is about taking care of those in your charge.

—SIMON SINEK

In education, we are really good at grabbing on to catchphrases and using them incessantly until teachers are begging us to put a phrase to rest. A popular catchphrase over the past few years is "building capacity." It is sometimes used in relation to professional learning, and it is sometimes used in relation to developing leadership skills. Although it is used in many different contexts, the essence of "building capacity" is the idea of learning in such a way that fosters independence. What if, instead, we believe the capacity is already there, and rather than focusing on building it, we talk about supporting our teachers in *accessing* their full capacity. The talent is present in the educators in your school. The job of a principal is to support teachers in accessing their capacity to do incredible work for the benefit of students. The job of a principal is to cultivate the talent that exists in the educators in their schools.

The most valuable commodity in any school is the collective wisdom of the educators, and the answers to all of our challenges are there, waiting for us to uncover them together.

I often tell stories of my shortcomings as a means of sharing my learning and growth. I am a work in progress, always, and I admire humbleness in others and try to be a leader who exemplifies both humbleness and confidence. However, sometimes a compliment can teach us as much as criticism, so I will share one of the greatest compliments I ever received with you. It

> **The most valuable commodity in any school is the collective wisdom of the educators, and the answers to all of our challenges are there, waiting for us to uncover them together.**

came in the form of a Facebook post by one of my quietest teachers. As I was leaving my last principalship, a teacher posted a picture of me and wrote, *It's rare I put anything out there like this, but here goes. See this beautiful soul? She might not know it but she has had one of the biggest impacts in my life of anyone I've ever met. She finds the best in you and somehow helps a person believe it.* That is our job, my principal friends. One of the most important jobs of a principal is to find the best in each staff member and help the staff member see it too and believe in themselves.

Cultivating Collective Talent

I joke that if principals want to describe themselves as being a particular kind of leader, like an instructional leader or a learning leader or an overwhelmed leader (wait, scratch that last one!), the most impactful title for a principal would be "collective efficacy leader." Rachel Eells's 2011 meta-analysis synthesized the results from twenty-six different studies and found that collective teacher efficacy is strongly and closely tied to student academic achievement.[12] Those who have been part of a team of teachers who know they serve students better because of their work together are not surprised by these findings. It is powerful when we are willing to look at data and evidence, understand what is working and what isn't, and work together to share strategies and improve instructional practices that meet the needs of students.

We so often mistake shared planning time or meeting frequently as collective efficacy. However, the reality is that the necessary vulnerable, transparent, and trusting relationships are often not established among the teachers on the team. Additionally, the focus on pedagogy and evidence of student learning is frequently not present during meetings. I have the honor to travel the country and coach teacher teams and school leaders from coast to coast, and I have witnessed this trend firsthand. Leaders and teachers have great intention to capitalize on collective efficacy, but what is missing is the shared understanding of what collective efficacy really is and how to achieve it.

Self-efficacy is the belief in your own ability to affect positive change. For example, a teacher might identify a challenge with getting the fourth-period class to engage in classroom discussions. A self-efficacious teacher would say something like, "So, I am going to try this strategy and collect evidence, then delve into the impact and next steps." A teacher with low self-efficacy might instead say, "I have no idea how to fix this problem. I've tried everything."

Collective efficacy is the belief that you can affect positive change best when you work as a team. It is firmly believing that when you have a challenge, you can always turn to your team for help and possible solutions. It is knowing the collective expertise present in the educators on your team can solve any problem.

As I talk with leaders and teachers, one of the most discouraging things in schools right now is that we want to fix everything all at once. This results in not doing anything very well and feeling guilty about it. We are much better off focusing our efforts on a few initiatives to ensure a deep level of implementation. Any initiative is significantly improved with teachers' collective efficacy because teachers will have ownership and lean on each other for support. Here are three basic things to think about as you are creating a school environment of interdependency.

1. **Establish trusting relationships within the teams.** One of the best ways to start a conversation about effective teaming is to talk about the difference between groups and teams, and the late Rick DuFour illustrated this concept so well by comparing marathon runners with a basketball team.[13] The marathon runners share the same goal, but no one would call them a team. They are a group of runners. The basketball team is a team in the truest sense, because they share a common goal and are dependent on each other to reach the goal. No one on a basketball team wins unless they all win. Rick was a pioneer in the idea of teachers' collective efficacy with his phenomenal PLC work. After you establish the true meaning of team together, lead the team to reflect individually on what they need from their team to do their best work. Then, support them in sharing what they need with each other. Record the list of what they need so they can refer back to it as the team establishes norms (behaviors expected from every team member during the meetings) for their team meetings. I agree with George's concept that one important norm is to engage in learning like we expect our students to, but this is where my thinking differs from George's around norms. I have seen the power of team norms when they are created by the team and lived out in every team meeting.

2. **Create a shared definition of teachers' collective efficacy.** Collaborating with teachers around what collective efficacy looks like and sounds like is important. Success criteria for this deep level of collaboration is crucial because it helps

teams determine their strengths and next steps. Here are some questions that can help teachers create this shared definition:

- What does collective efficacy look like during team meetings?

- What does it look like when your students are struggling with a concept and another teacher's students are mastering it? How about vice versa?

- What systems might we create together to support the focus on instruction and evidence of student learning?

- How can we carry the focus on pedagogy throughout the school year, even when we get busy with field trips, holiday events, P/T conferences, report cards, state testing, etc.?

- How can team discussions around learning, assessment, enrichment, and support help us stay focused on educational inquiry that fosters productive learning?

3. **Schedule team meetings and provide a coach.** We have to create time for team meetings to occur and hold that time sacred. Options include shared planning time, early release or late start days, afterschool meetings, getting rotating substitute teachers, etc. There are logistical issues to consider that are unique to every district, but (sorry to be blunt here) all scheduling efforts will fail if team meetings are not prioritized above all else. And then, after we have the team meeting time scheduled as firm as tungsten, we have to scaffold support so the time is used to collaborate on evidence of student learning and instruction. Just like with implementing any new thing, this is a process, and teacher teams will greatly benefit from having a dedicated coach to support them during their meetings. The coach can facilitate the meetings at first and then can gradually release the facilitation of the meetings to teachers on the team and be more of a "guide on the side" as

the culture of teacher collective efficacy becomes interwoven into the fabric of the school.

I am gifted with a unique perspective on schools, instruction, and learning because I work with so many different educators across the county. I believe more than ever that supporting teachers in the type of teaming described here and throughout the work of educational researchers is where our focus needs to be. This is not only because of the impact this collective work can have on student achievement, it is also because of the job satisfaction it creates for teachers. This is *exactly* the work they went into education for—they want to have a profound impact on student learning, and they know that dissecting percentages on a standardized state assessment does not help them improve instructional practices tomorrow for their students. After they understand the process, they cherish the time together to look at what their students can do and what their next steps are. They love sharing effective instructional strategies that work for the students in their school. Creating a culture of teachers' collective efficacy is a win-win and is so worthy of our dedicated focus.

Principals as Talent Coaches

One of my most popular blog posts was called "Principals: You Don't Need to Be an Instructional Leader." Although not intended, the title was a little click-baitish. Some readers of the post pushed back at me, saying, "Wait, this article is all about being an instructional leader!" Those readers had a point because the strategies I suggested in the article definitely support instruction and learning. However, my purpose in writing the article was to develop realistic expectations for principals as leaders of instruction.

Principals *cannot* be masters of best practices and pedagogy in every content area and every grade level. It is not possible, and it is not the best use of principal time and influence. School leaders instead should be focused on coaching teachers and support staff to develop their talents and to share their skills and wisdom with their colleagues.

Let's consider this quote from Rick DuFour and Mike Mattos:

> As former social studies teachers, we were not prepared to help a Spanish teacher improve when we couldn't understand what he/she was saying. We were ill-equipped to enhance the pedagogy of an industrial arts teacher when we were mechanically inept.[14]

We can all relate to this, can't we? DuFour and Mattos go on to explain that because they often couldn't assess whether the content or level of rigor in teaching was suitable, they had to rely on general monitoring of teaching quality and apply their knowledge of impactful questioning, authentic engagement, management strategies, and other related factors.

Raise your hand if you completely understand what they are talking about here. (I am having trouble typing right now because my right hand is high in the air.) I would often complete a teacher observation for our evaluation system and wonder how I was going to fulfill my promise to make the observation feedback valuable for the teacher. Maybe this is why research continually finds that teacher evaluation systems have zero or very little positive impact on student achievement?[15]

So, how can we leverage teacher observations, classroom walkthroughs, and other leadership behaviors to coach teachers and cultivate talent? Here are some dos and a few don'ts for educational leaders.

- **Have conversations with teachers about instruction**, not to evaluate them or give them guidance, but to learn from them as the pedagogy experts of their students. You can also use this time to understand their strengths and goals better so you can support them in their next steps. These conversations can be part of your feedback discussion after an observation, as you walk through classrooms before or after school, or scheduled conversations. Keep the conversations open-ended and directed by their goals by asking them questions like these:

- What student learning are you excited about right now?
- What instructional resource is really helping your students grow?
- Tell me about an instructional fail you recently had, and what did you learn from it?
- Where do you feel really strong instructionally?
- Where are you feeling weak instructionally, and how can I support your growth?
- What is one achievement you hope for students between now and the end of the quarter?

- **Always bring the conversation back to talking about evidence of student learning.** We can have thousands of the best curriculum resources at our fingertips, but not a single one of them matters if they are not positively impacting student learning. Teachers are great at planning together. They problem-solve student behavior issues, they align where they are in units, and they are master collaborative event planners. However, they are not always quick to pull out student work and sort through it together to look for strengths and next instructional steps. They need constant guidance and modeling from leaders to always bring the conversation back to evidence of student learning, and not just quarterly to look at percentages on standardized tests. This also gives us an opportunity to have teachers share effective instructional strategies with each other.

- **Shadow students.** Getting into classrooms frequently is imperative for effective school leadership. One of the best ways to understand what the student experience is in your school is to shadow students. There is no better way to learn what is working for students and what isn't working for them than to experience a day as they experience it. Ideally, you would do this frequently enough that you are able to experience student life in every grade level, with every teacher, and in every content area. It doesn't have to be a whole day; it can be helpful to shadow a student for part of a day.

- **Visit classrooms to leave positive feedback.** Want to gain a better understanding of what is happening in classrooms and build relationships and empower teachers at the same time? Visit classrooms with the singular purpose of leaving a positive handwritten note behind. Just like with students, teachers appreciate specific positive feedback. One way to do that is to leave cause-and-effect statements. Here is an example: *When you had students stand and use gestures to represent the vocabulary words, all of them became engaged again and excitedly participated.* Don't use classroom walkthroughs as gotchas for teachers. Not only will teachers cringe when you walk into their classrooms, there is research that says principal classroom walkthroughs can have a negative effect on student achievement when there is not a trusting environment and a shared understanding of the purpose of the walkthroughs.

- **Assign effective mentors.** Often mentor programs are one of those things we have in schools but don't invest much into. This is a missed opportunity for reciprocal learning for both the new teacher and the mentor. Effective mentors are vulnerable learners and skilled teachers, always looking for strengths, and they want to foster independence. What better way to cultivate talent than to pair mentor teachers with new teachers very strategically?

Great principals build systems and structures that support growth through identifying talents, building collective efficacy, and coaching and feedback to help educators access their full capacity. In turn, great teachers do the same thing for their students. When students and staff feel seen and valued, they feel like they can conquer the world. When principals help teachers see the value in each other, the sky's the limit for student learning.

3 QUESTIONS FOR CONVERSATION AND REFLECTION

1. How would you define collective efficacy, and what is in place in your school to nurture it? What might be a next step for your teams?
2. Finding the best in others and helping them believe it takes intentional action. What could you do more of to make this happen, and what could you do less of?
3. Which action idea did you most connect with in this chapter, and how might you want to adopt or adapt it?

CHAPTER 10

Shine Your Light and Get Out of My Way

BY ABBY RAMOS STANUTZ

As we let our light shine, we unconsciously give other people permission to do the same. As we are liberated from our own fear, our presence actually liberates others.

—MARIANNE WILLIAMSON

There was a lot I liked about working with Matt Warnock. I liked that his meetings always had agendas, and he would cover teachers' classes himself if their kid got pinkeye or the flu. We—students and staff—loved that he dressed up as the Elf on a Shelf during the holidays, rode his skateboard from class to class, and did the worm at school dances, even though we begged him to stop. Lots of principals are likable or charming, but few take that goodwill and turn it into an environment of continuous growth and inspiration. Those of us who worked for Matt knew that we had the power to transform students' lives, and that fire lit us from within.

Much to his secretary's dismay, the door of his office was literally always open, whether he was in or out. It was not unusual to see a teacher sitting crumpled in an armchair waiting for him to return from his rounds. I sat there many times, first with trepidation about what he may say and then, later, excited about some new idea I had for promoting literacy on my campus. I'd never before had that level of empowerment on a campus. I was a good teacher, but he made me a great one by shining a light on everything I had to offer kids and then, frankly, by getting out of my way.

During the pandemic, like many teachers, I struggled with hybrid teaching. I missed the connection to my students, I worried for their safety, and I was incredibly concerned about the lack of reading material in their homes. Our Title 1 urban suburban campus looked as state-of-the-art as any in upper-class America, but it was a facade disguising extreme poverty and need. A good number of our students were packed into apartment buildings furnished only with a mattress or a "cardboard dresser." Several others were essentially homeless, living indefinitely in extended-stay hotels. On one first day of school survey, a student wrote *cereal box* when I asked what they had to read in their home. Our students were among the hardest-hit populations in the state of Texas by the pandemic, so I could also imagine the fear that students felt during that difficult time. After a particularly sleepless night, I stormed into Matt's office and announced, "I am going to get books out to the kids in our school, and I need your help."

Legs crossed and brow furrowed, he very patiently let me explain my idea for a bi-weekly book drive-thru and book delivery service in which masked teachers would drop freezer bags full of books on student doorsteps. In short, I was proposing a logistical nightmare. Most principals would have patted me on the head, commended my big

> **I was a good teacher, but he made me a great one by shining a light on everything I had to offer kids and then, frankly, by getting out of my way.**

heart, and explained that it was just too much. Too much work in an already stressful time with no quantifiable benefit. Instead, he never asked me if this would have a positive effect on standardized test scores or how I was planning to measure success. Instead, he once again said, "Make it happen," and he let me get to work.

What is extraordinary is that this type of initiative was not uncommon on our campus. *Making it happen* became the culture on our campus, first through his support and then in the way we empowered each other as teachers. When the leader of a school clearly states that we will always do what is best for kids and stands behind those words daily, the inspiration is infectious.

It may surprise you to hear that when this new principal introduced himself to the staff, I was prepared to hate him. I know this sounds harsh, but what you have to know about me is that I have always taken this job very seriously and have zero patience for people who do not. Or in this case, those who I *think* do not understand the gravity of our profession. As soon as the change in admin was unceremoniously announced at a monthly faculty meeting, the school vibrated with uncertainty. (Side note: We do not spend enough time acknowledging the emotional trauma of changing principals, but that is for another time.) At this point, I had already been in the game long enough to know what a new principal means for teachers: new initiatives, new responsibilities, new paperwork, and new demands. I was skeptical at best.

So how did he become the most inspirational person in my educational career? He disagreed with me.

Not to honk my own horn, but I am the kind of teacher who has always succeeded. You know the type: the kind of teacher that principals don't have to worry about. We make it to morning duty, our grades are submitted on time, and we rarely need your help. We feel most at home in our classrooms and are guided by the belief that teaching children is important work. So when he walked through the door to observe my class, I was expecting the glowing reviews I'd received countless times before: "Keep up the good work!" "Great rapport with the kids!" "You're an engaging teacher!"

This, however, was not the case.

Instead, he had the audacity to ask me, "Do they ever do anything except read?"

I was dumbfounded. *Does he know who I am? I'm the best teacher in this school. Ask anyone!*

I thought about that question for days. As a language and literature teacher, I had a myriad of reasons for the amount of reading we were doing in class, but the question plagued me like a paper cut. I furiously reexamined my entire practice, turned over every lesson, and justified my reasoning for the choices I made. Later that month, he asked me to come in and have a chat about a project I had been assigning for a few years, an adorable family tree poster where students were asked to research their own names and backgrounds. Through the course of the conversation, I slowly saw the project in a new light: a cutesy, possibly problematic activity not especially aligned to any standards. Still, he never told me outright the issues with the project. If anything, he complimented all of the effort and thought I'd put into the expectations. He told me I was free to make any choices I saw fit in my classroom, smiled, and ushered me out.

Walking back to my room clutching those family trees, it all clicked. The answers to the questions weren't important to him at all—they were for me. He saw the good teacher I was and was pointing me toward the great teacher I could be. From that moment forward, I knew the expectations would be different for us all. We would be held to a new standard. Almost all of my colleagues have a similar story. He saw the unique talents of each teacher in the building, shined a light on the areas where we had room for growth, and then got out of our way to watch us make it happen.

Throughout the ten years he led our campus, it became a common understanding that we were always trying to be the best teachers we could for every student in the building, whether they were on our roll or not. I'd heard this idea in theory but never seen it blossom on a campus. Throughout the years, teachers felt empowered to take risks, because the choices in our classrooms were our own, so there was no shame or fear in a spontaneous observation. We were excited to show off, and any feedback felt helpful instead of insulting. The open office door policy translated to the understanding that all staff were welcome in every room in the building because the students were all "our" students. We observed each other frequently, in structured and unstructured ways. We left feedback and encouragement with Post-its and scraps of paper in our boxes. *Thanks for letting me join your class today. I needed inspiration! PS Padlet would be great for that reflection part.*

If a department organized an event, the others joined in to help. When I launched the book drive-through, teachers from all disciplines worked the tent, delivered books, and raised money to buy reading materials for kids. Like on any campus, it was not always harmonious. We know passionate educators will not always agree. There were heated discussions, slammed doors, and tearful debates. The difference, however, was that each one of us felt our opinion was respected, our voice was important, the autonomy in our classroom was protected, and the direction of the school was truly in all of our hands. Through this empowerment, we all became better teachers day by day. We felt collectively responsible for each student's success and also the success of each teacher on our team.

A great principal is a person who *empowers* teachers to be the best they can be. A leader who really cares about the teaching and the relationships above all else. Someone who holds back the paperwork avalanche so teachers are allowed to stretch and grow. Over the years, we teachers have wanted a lot of things from administrators, but I truly believe that the best way to cultivate talent is to give your staff is the power to "make it happen."

3 QUESTIONS FOR CONVERSATION AND REFLECTION

1 Do you have an open-door policy? Why or why not?

2 What is the culture of feedback on your campus? What ideas did you take away from this chapter about feedback?

3 How do you encourage teachers to grow, create, and take risks? How much agency do teachers on your campus have?

CHAPTER 11

Empowering Teacher Leaders

BY DR. RYAN DANIEL

The best leaders are those most interested in surrounding themselves with assistants and associates smarter than they are.

—JOHN C. MAXWELL

When I was an assistant principal, I really appreciated that there were two of us assistant principals on the administrative team. My partner handled discipline, and my focus was instruction. Together we were the perfect Robin for our Batman, our principal. During that time in my life, I would journal and write down all of the different ways I would utilize my assistant principal to leverage my leadership when I became a principal.

Boy, was I quite surprised when I was appointed as a principal and had no assistant principal my first year. I didn't even realize this was a thing. How could I run an entire school building alone? Who was going to be my thought partner? How was I going to support instruction, answer emails, handle discipline, and build relationships with everyone? I was doomed.

I remember my first year as a principal there was a teacher leader who had served in the capacity of the "silent principal" with the previous principal. She was not a leader by official title, but she knew the ins and outs of the school building, was respected by all, and had access to everything. She was amazing, she knew instruction, and she knew pedagogy. I was honestly quite intimidated by her. And she was not all that impressed with me and didn't think I would last longer than a year. We struggled to understand each other in the beginning; we just couldn't find our groove together.

During our first meeting, I asked her what her strength was, what subject she felt she was the best at. Immediately I could tell by her demeanor that I'd offended her with the question. She did it all and had strengths in many areas; she thought I was implying that she was strong in only one area. However, my intent was to streamline the support she provided to teachers so I could better support her. She told me that she did it all, both reading and math. I asked her if she had to choose one to focus on, what would it be, and she finally said reading. I told her that from that point forward, her focus was reading and that I would handle math. She became the reading lead teacher, and our roller coaster together began.

This interaction was a big lesson for me, and I learned that people buy into the person, not the position. Just because I was the principal, it didn't automatically make people jump on the bus with me.

In my eight years of being a school leader, I have never had the opportunity to have an assistant principal. Operating a school as a single administrator has taught me the value in cultivating teacher leaders. A culture of leadership is far more powerful than a book of policies. My first year as a principal forced me to recognize the silent leaders in the building and the loud role they play in moving instruction and sustaining a positive school

> **A culture of leadership is far more powerful than a book of policies.**

culture. As my reading lead teacher taught me more about the curriculum, I watched her support teachers in different capacities around the school, and I observed how committed and dedicated she was to our school community. For her, it didn't matter who was leading the building; she was going to do whatever needed to be done to ensure our school was successful. But I also observed how exhausted she was, doing it alone, and I paid attention to her desire to have a thought partner. I quietly watched her wanting to learn and develop her own leadership skills. I wanted to support her, and I wanted to be her thought partner. I also wanted her support for my leadership vision.

Principals play a crucial role in cultivating talent among their staff. Fostering an environment that promotes personal and professional growth is essential for nurturing talent. The reality is that principals can't do everything on their own. Teacher leaders can share the responsibility of school leadership, creating a distributed leadership model. Not only does this lighten the workload of the principal but also allows for a more collaborative and inclusive approach to decision-making and problem-solving. Here I was trying to run a school by myself when the reality was I had a Robin, I was just looking for it in an assistant principal, not a teacher leader.

So how do you empower those silent but loud teacher leaders, who may or may not have an official leadership title? Often, as principals, we believe that by giving someone else the power to be in charge or control an area we lose our power as the principal. It's not the position that gives you power; it's how you make people feel when they're around you that gives you that power. Great principals understand that their role is to support students, but in order to support students, they have to empower teachers.

Some of the key action steps I took to empower my teacher leader were:

1. **Identify the strengths of teacher leaders.** My teacher leader knew what she was consistently responsible for, but she wasn't

sure what her biggest strength was. Together we talked about the areas that she felt the most comfortable in and identified gaps in her leadership that she wanted to grow in.

2. **Value what teacher leaders bring to the table.** Oftentimes, as school leaders, we believe we are the smartest person in the room. I constantly made sure my teacher leader knew I was learning from her, and I was careful to consult her anytime I had a reading question. It didn't diminish my capacity to support reading in our school, but it allowed her to constantly thrive in an area that was a strength for her.

3. **Define the roles.** Being a teacher leader is frequently a gray area. Defining her role as a teacher leader and my role in how I was going to support her allowed our relationship to be intentional. Confusion is eliminated when roles are defined. Enlisting feedback from your teacher leaders about what their role is also creates a culture of collaboration.

4. **Encourage collaboration and shared decision-making.** Her opinions mattered, and I made sure she knew that by including her in conversations and decision-making. I ensured she had a seat at the table but also supported her while she was there. Teacher leaders thrive in environments where they are given the opportunity to be a part of the conversation. When teachers are actively engaged in shaping the direction of the school, they are more invested in its success and more motivated to contribute their best efforts.

5. **Be THE leader.** A teacher leader still wants direction. Very similar to a high-performing student, they know the expectations and receive the message "Go, be great. I know you can do it!" But when do we support them? When do we encourage them? This scenario is the same for the high-performing teacher and teacher leader. Because we know what they are capable of, we sometimes forget to lead them. We give them the task, and we just let them go. Teacher leaders want guidance

and direction as well. In order for them to be empowered by you, they have to know and understand that you are capable of leading them.

6. **Provide feedback.** In order to cultivate talent and empower teacher leaders, you need to let them know how well (or not) they are doing. Framing your feedback in a format where the teacher leader can grow will create a culture of continuous improvement.

Teacher leadership is essential for principals because it not only supports instructional improvement but also strengthens the school's overall culture and effectiveness. My relationship with my reading lead teacher is probably one of the strongest I have with any teacher who has worked with me. Even now, after I have transitioned to another school, we talk often, being each other's thought partners. I remember when I left my first school, she took the news the hardest. I believe our relationship grew so strong because I was intentional about how I supported and empowered her. As principals, it is important that we recognize and foster teacher leadership strategically and very intentionally. Remember, it's not the position that makes you powerful, it's how you make people feel—the power that you instill in others—that makes you a great principal.

3 QUESTIONS FOR CONVERSATION AND REFLECTION

1 Who are the teacher leaders in your school, and how do you support and empower them?

2 Dr. Daniel identified the importance of principals having at least one thought partner in the building. Who is your thought partner, and how do you nurture that relationship?

3 Which key action step from this chapter did you connect with, and how will you put it into practice right away?

CHAPTER 12

I Still Can't Believe What Happened

BY VINCENT TAYLOR

If you're not prepared to be wrong, you'll never come up with anything original.

—KEN ROBINSON

We have all uttered that familiar phrase before, "Actions speak louder than words." Just think about that time when you were made a promise by someone who vowed to do something for you. As much as you wanted to believe them, those five words subconsciously seeped into your mind as they declared their word to you, yet never followed through. "Actions speak louder than words." It means the same thing today as it did eight hundred years ago when St. Anthony of Padua first said it. During my twenty-eight years as a teacher, I have heard those words voiced by numerous individuals about their principals. However, I work for a principal who has unequivocally proven year after year that her word is her bond. This is the same principal who empowers her teachers to share their gifts with others in an effort to help students and staff grow. She is a talent cultivator through and through.

I can remember it like it was yesterday. I sat across the table from the entire leadership team after we observed a fourth-grade lesson together. We were sharing strengths and next steps in our instruction following the observation. Mrs. McKinney, a principal of eighteen years, knew I had developed an affinity for creating instructional frameworks. However, due to my shyness and reluctance to verbally share my innovations, I simply sat quietly as the academic discourse continued. Determined to break this cycle that I had become complacent with, Mrs. McKinney shined a spotlight on me by asking for my feedback. I could sense by the way she was looking at me that she knew I really wanted to share my idea.

"Mr. Taylor, what do you think?" she asked, giving me the perfect opportunity to expound on a best practice idea that I had come up with over a month earlier. "How would you address what you saw in the lesson?" she asked. Even though I had knots in my stomach from the anxiety of answering her, I knew this was my time. Hands trembling while a film of sweat covered my forehead, I reached inside my manila folder and slowly pulled out a multicolored diagram that illustrated a comprehensive instructional framework. It delved into the time-management aspect of a lesson while also considering the systematic flow of the Gradual Release of Responsibility model. I handed her a freshly printed copy to peruse.

As she analyzed every word on the paper, I waited anxiously to hear her thoughts. After a few seconds, her face showed not even the slight expression. Just as I began to feel defeated, she displayed what resembled a smile. I did not quite know how to read how she truly felt. But then it happened, a full-fledged smile. "Oh my gosh!" she said. "Did you create this, Mr. Taylor?" Immediately, she began sharing various components of the instructional framework with everyone at the table. Her infectious enthusiasm spread throughout the entire room. She loved my contribution and made no secret about it.

I was ecstatic over her response but even more so about her willingness to share her excitement with everyone. It is fair to say we all have experienced, or have a friend who has experienced, a principal who, unfortunately, does not celebrate their teachers' talents. If the idea was not conceived by them, then it does not hold as much importance. Well, luckily, I work with an administrator who champions her staff. If she does not know the answer to a particular question, she has no qualms about consulting her team for assistance. She possesses a trait that is invaluable, and that is transparency. Also, when she is showered with compliments regarding the performance of the school, she instantly says things like, "I could not have done this without my team" or "I'm fortunate to have the team that I do." Still elated about her approval, I grinned, trying to maintain my composure. Well, the adulation did not stop there. She asked if I could share my information with all the teachers during our schoolwide professional development. Honored by this request, I smiled again, shaking my head in disbelief. On that Tuesday, I went home feeling empowered, knowing that my contribution would not only help teachers at my school but that it was valued by my educational leader.

I couldn't believe what happened.

A few days passed, and I was still on cloud nine. While on my lunch break, the intercom sounded. "Mr. Taylor, please come to the principal's office." Now, as you can imagine, I was wondering why I was being called to the office. Quickly, I searched my mental database to see if I could recall anything out of the ordinary that happened that day. As I racked my brain, I left Room 14 to head her way. As soon as I walked out of my classroom, I was accosted by three of my coworkers, who blurted out, "You know Mrs. McKinney wants to see you?" Of course, now I was even more anxious than before.

As I entered her office, she immediately told me to have a seat. There was an awkward silence that filled the room as her laser-focused eyes pierced the content on her three-monitor computer setup. So, I just stared at the ceiling, waiting in suspense. A few seconds later, she turned to me, emulating the same enthusiastic energy she had the day I initially shared my plan. Smiling once more, she expressed how much she loved my idea. "I wanted to let you know that I shared your work with my cohort of principals, and they all loved it!" she said excitedly. So, in addition to Cedar Hills Elementary, there were now eight additional schools that would be implementing a resource I created. I was in awe. This was not what I envisioned when I hesitantly shared my framework a few days ago. As a quiet and reserved teacher, I never sought to have the spotlight. But I must admit, it felt great knowing that my principal saw something in me and refused to let me hide under my insecurities and let a great instructional strategy go unknown. Through her numerous acknowledgments, she empowered me by valuing my contribution and sharing it with as many people as she could.

So, yes, we all know at least one person who will claim to do extraordinary things for us, promising us the world, only to disappoint us time after time. I cannot speak for everyone, but I know one thing for sure: Marva McKinney is the epitome of the phrase "Actions speak louder than words." Being a leader of integrity is the first step to building a trusting environment that allows talent to shine. Mrs. McKinney saw something in me and supported me in sharing my talents with other educators. Here are a few of the things she did to cultivate talent at our school.

> **It felt great knowing that my principal saw something in me and refused to let me hide under my insecurities and let a great instructional strategy go unknown.**

- She had a structure in place that allowed teachers an opportunity to collaborate and share their talents. This was through teachers observing each other, learning alongside each other, and building leadership.
- She gave credit where credit was due. Rather than taking accolades for herself, she continuously turned praise back to

her team. This empowered us to recognize our strengths and to share our talents.

- She sought out ways for teachers to shine and pushed us to share our skills and wisdom.

3 QUESTIONS FOR CONVERSATION AND REFLECTION

1 What structures do you have in place that give teachers an opportunity to share their talents?

2 What are the various ways you celebrate your teachers' talents?

3 How do you extract the talents from a teacher who is an introvert?

PILLAR FOUR
Resource Maximizer

Great principals work hard to maximize the resources they have in their schools, and this includes human resources, curricular resources, systems, time, and money. Principals are resource maximizers when they are clear on the vision and match resources with the goals of the school, constantly reflecting and collaborating to make sure they are maximized. School leaders realize that effective systems can support the maximization of resources and work alongside staff to develop and refine systems to meet the needs of the school community.

PREFACE
Leading Needs Managing

BY GEORGE COUROS

One of the most important tasks of a manager is to eliminate people's excuses for failure.

—ROBERT TOWNSEND, *UP THE ORGANIZATION*

You often hear this sentiment in and out of education: "We don't need managers; we need leaders!"

It is imperative that you have people who can do both.

Stephen Covey shared, "Leadership is about people, management is about things." You can have all the vision in the world, but if you aren't able to put the *things* in the hands of the people you serve, it is impossible to be truly effective.

The pillar "Resource Maximizer" is about how we give people the opportunity to do the things they need to be successful in their work.

It isn't the most exciting thing to discuss, but it doesn't make it any less critical. And far too often, people don't get the credit they deserve for removing barriers that keep people from being able to be effective in their work. Case in point: When was the last time you called your

IT department and said, "Hey! The internet worked all day! Thank you!" We often hear that people don't have what they need, but when everything is accessible, we really don't notice.

Time Is Also a Resource Where Attention Is Needed

How we utilize time can be a barrier to success.

Here is an example: no matter which decade you were in when you were in school as a student, whether it was the 1960s or the 2020s, the length of the school day was pretty much the same, give or take a few minutes. Yet, what we ask teachers to do continues to grow and involves more and more of their time each year.

As the kids say, the math ain't mathing.

The role of a great administrator is to help move things forward while also being able to ask, "What do we no longer need to do?"

For every initiative added, something needs to go. Not only is this the only way to move forward, it is also the only way to keep up—at minimum.

So, how do we decide what needs to go?

We ask.

If you are considering trying something new in your school, ask the people you serve what they believe is no longer needed.

And if the answer is, "Well, there is nothing that we are doing currently that we can feasibly get rid of," then maybe the answer becomes not to take on that new initiative or idea.

If we want to evolve our practices to align with the world we live in, it doesn't necessarily mean we need to do more. It often means that we have to understand what is working that we can strengthen, what isn't working that we can leave behind, and what is possible to meet the needs of all learners.

To Make Spaces Better, Be in Those Spaces

So, how can principals make better decisions for our classrooms?

If you are in a role that makes decisions for what the environment looks like in a classroom, you need to be present in those classrooms.

It is as simple as that.

So how do we do that?

As a principal way back in the early aughts (the early 2000s), I had a laptop. It weighed about ninety-five pounds more than the one I have now, but I had it. And what that meant was that I wasn't tethered to a wall.

I would take advantage of that by asking a teacher if I could sit in the back of their classroom and knock out some emails. I wouldn't simply do the walkthrough, or what

> If you are in a role that makes decisions for what the environment looks like in a classroom, you need to be present in those classrooms.

I call the "superintendent entourage" (you know what I am talking about), but would park myself at a table or desk in a classroom. It was clearly communicated to the teacher what I was doing. I would say, "I am not here to observe you; I am here to observe the environment we are putting you in and see how we can support you best."

In one case, I remember a teacher wanting to use iPads with her students, and the Wi-Fi wasn't working great. What did she do? The same thing so many educators have done over the years, even though there is no evidence it has ever worked in the history of the internet.

She stood up on a chair, got on a desk, and, as if she was in Cirque du Soleil, she delicately balanced herself and raised the iPad skyward in hopes that Thor, the God of Thunder (and possibly Wi-Fi) would magically hit that iPad with a bolt of internet.

Nada.

As I watched this unfold, I called our central office IT department and said, "Hey . . . I am watching a teacher right now unable to get internet access for her or her students, so we need more access points in this room, or no one will be able to use these devices effectively. Can you have someone come down and help us out?"

Back on solid ground, she looked at me and mouthed, "Thank you."

Within twenty-four hours, the IT department had added some access points and removed that barrier that she was literally willing to become a P. T. Barnum circus performer to overcome, and everyone felt better.

Moving Forward

Teachers face barriers far too often, and many times, we hear nothing because so many great teachers don't want to *bother* their administrators. I distinctly remember saying to my staff, "I cannot fix problems that I don't know exist, so always let me know if I can help." This wasn't limited to the "things" we needed, but any other problems that were happening in our schools. But it definitely did not exclude resources.

The best way to know about obstacles you can help your teachers overcome is by being in classrooms as often as possible.

If we want what is best for our students, we have to do whatever we can to remove barriers and be thoughtful about what is needed to help our teachers and staff be as successful as possible.

Remember, leadership is about people, and management is about things.

To help our people, we have to pay attention to the time and resources to which they have access.

CHAPTER 13

Resource Maximizer

BY ALLYSON APSEY

Management is doing things right; leadership is doing the right things.

—PETER F. DRUCKER

If you consider yourself a servant-leader, do either of these scenarios ring true for you?

The **"chicken with your head cut off"** servant-leader: This type of leader runs around doing all the jobs and solving all the problems, all day, every day. At the end of the day, the leader looks over her own to-do list and despairs that she has not crossed a single thing off. She accepts that she will yet again burn the midnight oil to keep her head above water. It often feels like no one can solve a problem without hand-holding, as if they lack the confidence to make any decision without her stamp of approval.

The **"I prefer to do things myself rather than delegate because it is easier and it gets done right"** servant-leader: This type of servant-leader fears adding too much to the workload of staff and ends up spending his days doing things that could be accomplished by others. He wonders why the district leadership is always griping at him for missing deadlines—how can he be expected to do his own job when he is doing everyone else's? Occasionally he feels like a hero after hours of inputting student data into a new program or single-handedly setting up for a school event, but mostly he feels defeated and overwhelmed.

Full disclosure: I have been both of these types of leaders at certain points in my career. And it has me wondering: Is servant leadership misunderstood in education? And how might educational leaders maximize resources with servant leadership to empower others and truly lead?

The idea of servant leadership is not a new concept; in fact, it's over fifty years old. The management style was first described by Robert K. Greenleaf, founder of the modern servant leadership movement, in a 1970 essay. Here is how Greenleaf defined the servant-leader: "Servant leadership always empathizes, always accepts the person, but sometimes refuses to accept some of the person's effort or performance as good enough."[16] Servant leadership is not about doing others' work or accepting poor performance; it is quite the opposite. It is about understanding and believing in your people enough that you expect them to do great things.

As I read quotes from Greenleaf and others about servant leadership, it quickly becomes clear that the shift from traditional leadership to servant leadership is a shift from focusing on the product to focusing on the people. The reality is that the most expensive resource in a school district is staff salaries and benefits. In some districts, salaries and benefits account for more than 80 percent of the budget. The product and function of the organization do matter, but *the people* in the organization matter more. And research conducted about highly successful, people-focused businesses proves that focusing on the well-being of the people in your organization can lead to very successful and profitable outcomes. This was evidenced by a 2016 study that linked organization wellness efforts with an increase in stock profits, noting that "stock values for a portfolio of companies that received high scores in a corporate health and wellness self-assessment appreciated by 235% compared with the S&P 500 Index appreciation of 159% over a 6-year simulation period."[17]

In the trenches of the COVID pandemic, school principals had to roll up their sleeves and do whatever was necessary to keep their schools functioning as well as they could. Being a resource maximizer took on a whole different meaning. That meant subbing in classrooms, supervising recess, making attendance calls—you name it, we did it. And we would do it again in a heartbeat, whenever necessary. For servant-leaders, no role in the organization is beneath them, and it is necessary to walk the talk when needed.

Here is the quandary, though. If leaders are spending their days doing jobs other than leading, who is doing the leading? Who is listening to, empathizing with, and supporting staff? Who is providing feedback to staff that empowers their continuous growth? Who is maximizing all the resources available and accessing other needed resources? We all know the answer—no one. And where do organizations without leaders end up? In chaos. My principal friend Matt Dansby from

> **If leaders are spending their days doing jobs other than leading, who is doing the leading?**

Pickerington, Ohio, said it like this: "I am always willing to get into the trenches. I just need to get out as soon as possible to get back to the front line."

In the next chapter, Brad Gustafson will share ideas about building a system to budget for innovation, and I love his story because it represents out-of-the-box thinking about a system that was created decades ago. One of the ways to serve and maximize resources is to get really good at creating systems that work for what students and school communities need *today*. Now, systems will never solve every problem, but they support us in tapping into resources proactively. Systems can empower staff to know where to begin and what questions to ask. Here are a few systems leaders may want to consider setting up this school year if they are not already in place:

1. **Make your "mental checklists" visible.** Like you, most mornings my phone buzzed with a new text message right after I got out of bed (and sometimes before I got out of bed), alerting me to yet another staff shortage. For a while, I was the only person who could solve that problem. But then I decided to put my mental checklist down on paper, and it made all the difference. With the support of the checklist, my secretary or another staff member could work through the possible options to come up with a plan. When I was there, I was involved in the plan, but we always referred back to the checklist, even when I was right beside the staff member. That way, when I wasn't there, they had a habit of starting with the checklist.

   Making mental checklists visible could apply to any number of everyday problems you solve as a leader. And here is the bonus: these checklists don't just save you time, they support staff in feeling like they are proficient and empowered problem-solvers.

2. **Create a schedule for crisis response.** Are the same people always responding to crisis situations in your school? For us, when there was a crisis, typically the principal, the social worker, the school psychologist, at least one support staff person, and a resource room teacher would respond. Very infrequently did the level of crisis call for five people; usually the crisis could be resolved with just one person intervening. So, we created a "crisis response schedule" that had one person listed as the first responder. That person always had a walkie-talkie so they could get in touch with an additional support person quickly if necessary. We divided the schedule up by half days, and each of us took one or two half days per week. I was included on

the schedule, and, when it wasn't my turn, I was careful to not respond unless I was asked to. It was hard, but I needed to show staff that I had full confidence in their ability to de-escalate a crisis situation. And if I didn't have confidence in a particular staff member, that indicated to me that I had some work to do to help train that staff member appropriately.

3. **Develop an "only me" list.** There are a few things that only school leaders can do that cannot be delegated. For instance, it is the responsibility of leaders to complete evaluations and conduct observations, and this important leadership role cannot be passed on to someone else. What other responsibilities fall into this same category for you? Consider making an "only me" list to reflect back on daily, and determine if, each day, you had time to complete tasks that need to be done by only you or if your time was spent on things that could be done by others. Then, consider solutions that will allow you to spend time on your "only me" tasks, like the suggestions listed here of making mental checklists visible, developing a schedule to share the responsibility, or embracing the strengths of others by delegating.

4. **Tap into the strengths of others.** There are so many talents and strengths among the staff members on our campuses. You already know that. When you ask a staff member to help you problem-solve a challenge you are having and the problem is aligned with a strength they have, they will likely solve the problem better than you ever could. And being asked to help you is empowering and contributes to a culture of vulnerability and collaboration. Consider adding this question to the bottom of your "only me" list: Am I empowering others through their strengths?

5. **Leverage time for teacher collaboration.** We often hear educators talk about the lack of time for collaboration, thinking that it needs to fit within the thirty-minute staff meeting they

are allotted each month. Sometimes it takes getting very creative, like one school I work with that found some space in their PE teacher's schedule and worked teacher team meetings into those slots of time. Another school I work with created time by aligning middle school students' related arts class to give teams of teachers a regular opportunity to work together during the school day. What could we remove from teachers' schedules that would allow them to work together with a focus on student learning? Might students be better served if we replace things like traditional teacher committees with collaboration around evidence of learning and instruction?

All of us entered leadership to serve people, but if our focus is instead on serving tasks, the core focus of servant leadership is neglected. In addition, we will neglect valuable resources that are already available in our schools and miss the opportunity to learn what resources are needed. Let's give ourselves permission to be servant-leaders by focusing on the people we serve and prioritizing the things that only school or district leaders can do. Yes, we will do whatever it takes to help our schools and districts be successful, but let's be mindful that we are consciously out on the front line leading the way.

Managing Resources

Several years ago we collected cleaning supplies for a school in Michigan. Why cleaning supplies, you ask? Well, there was a district in Michigan getting a lot of press for the poor conditions of their school buildings. Our student leadership team wanted to do something to help another school in Michigan, so I found a principal who worked in the district with the deteriorating buildings and asked her what her school needed. She told me that there was a moratorium on purchasing supplies of any kind in the district, and she said they needed things like Clorox wipes, paper towels, and tissues. This was pre-COVID, if you can believe it.

The families in their community could not afford to purchase these items for the school, so we did.

My husband, sons, and I loaded up the back of our pickup truck with the piles of cleaning supplies the student leadership team collected and drove two hours to deliver them to the school. Their staff was so excited, and the kind principal gave me a tour of the school. The building was indeed in rough shape, and my heart broke for the students and the staff who had to deal with the falling-down ceilings and overall disrepair. The principal took me into classrooms, and at one point we walked through an unused classroom that was being used to store textbooks. Brand-new textbooks that were shelved because the district had decided to switch to a different curriculum resource. I could not believe my eyes—in that room were tens of thousands of dollars' worth of new books in this school that was not allowed to purchase basic cleaning supplies. Talk about mismanagement of resources.

Being a resource maximizer is a bit like Goldilocks, in that too many resources can be a barrier to progress, and too few resources can lead to misalignment between actions and goals. It is important that leaders help teachers, students, and the community have access to the resources that will allow them to accomplish student academic goals. This means that principals have to first understand the resources already available and the resources that are needed, and then advocate for their school community to get the necessary resources. This may come in the form of grant-writing, communicating clearly with the district office, and/or utilizing support like a parent-teacher organization.

Narrow and Align the Focus

We want to do everything all at once in schools because our work is urgent. We need our students to succeed in all academic areas, we need to create environments where they can thrive, and we need to equip them with life skills to be successful in whatever path they choose. It is challenging for educators to realize that when we try to do everything all at once, we do nothing well. Walter Isaacson, who wrote a biography of Steve Jobs, described the way Jobs led his team to focus on just three priorities. He wrapped up a retreat with the top one hundred leaders at Apple by asking them to identify the ten things they should be doing next, and then after they had been identified, he slashed the bottom seven from the list and said they would focus only on the top three.[18] Can you imagine doing that in a school setting, forgetting every initiative and focus area but the top three? Unfortunately, the answer is no. But if we want to make progress, we have to limit the number of initiatives.

We can narrow our focus by tackling the most pressing student needs first. Our students must be able to read and write, so that is a great place to start. In order to give educators permission to go all-in with the few most important initiatives, we also have to allow them to opt out of things that are not serving students or the community. We can move mountains together when we concentrate on just a few goals at a time.

Maximizing resources does not mean having the most resources, it means having the necessary resources. It means having the right resources to maximize learning. It means identifying all the resources that are currently at your disposal, especially the human resources in your school. This takes careful communication with all stakeholders, especially teachers.

3 QUESTIONS FOR CONVERSATION AND REFLECTION

1. What systems are you considering putting into place to maximize the human resources at your school? What will be your first step?

2 Which idea suggested in this chapter did you connect with, and why? Is there something you could stop doing in order to start implementing the new idea?

3 Talk a walk around your building to consider resources that are not being maximized. Are spaces, learning tools, or human resources being underutilized, and how could those resources be maximized?

CHAPTER 14

Align Resources with Your Vision

BY BRAD GUSTAFSON

The courage to imagine the otherwise is our greatest resource, adding color and suspense to all our life.

—DANIEL J. BOORSTIN

Everyone wants to be a maximizer on some level, whether we're talking about time, the budget, or elevating students and staff. We want to make a difference.

There are some things we don't want as well. We don't want to settle or miss important opportunities. And we certainly don't want to champion the status quo. But sometimes, this is exactly what we're doing.

I'm not proud to admit this, but I was in my seventh (or so) year as an elementary school principal when I realized I was doing something that was not helping our staff and students. I had this leadership epiphany when a teacher approached me after school to talk through an idea she had. It was almost the end of the school year. Therefore, the only thing tighter than everyone's schedule was our budget.

I'm embarrassed to admit this, but I don't even remember what the teacher was specifically asking for. But I do remember how she responded after our conversation—and it was heartbreaking. After I listened to her idea with genuine excitement, I encouraged her to consider seeking out grant funding or revisiting the idea the following school year when our supply budget was renewed. I also assured her that I'd look further into things to see if there was something we might be able to do.

The teacher politely accepted what I was sharing, but there was something about her response that reminded me of a balloon deflating. Maybe it was the way her shoulders slightly shrunk as I tried to explain our situation. Either way, I could tell from her body language how much she believed in our students—and that this idea would make a positive difference. The fact I had built a budget that couldn't support student-centered ideas in a more timely manner was heavy on my mind.

That evening, I was reflecting on the process I use for budgeting. It was the same process I had used for seven (or more) years. I would always take the previous year's budget, add or subtract dollars based on our allocation, and apply them to the same line items. Year after year. But why?!

What's even worse is that I'm pretty confident the budget I was rolling over from year to year had been created years before I was hired. This means it's not outside the realm of possibility I was submitting an annual budget created for students who went to school the previous decade . . . or even earlier. Think about that?!

After realizing we could do better—and should do better—we started reviewing the budget with a different perspective. To maximize our dollars, we knew we needed them to reflect our

> **To maximize our dollars, we knew we needed them to reflect our priorities and vision.**

priorities and vision. We also needed to be more nimble. When teachers approach us to request support for an idea that would improve student learning, we want to be in a position to say yes.

We added a line item to the budget called "Innovation." It was a modest amount, but it was also a stake in the ground. The line item represented our first step in taking tangible actions to better align our resources with our words and beliefs. In that moment, I resolved to stop asking educators to make meaningful changes to their practice without making meaningful changes to how I was approaching school finances. For the first time in a long time, I started approaching our budget with the posture of a resource maximizer instead of just a resource allocator.

The line item for "Innovation" continues to support our school-wide priorities—even as they evolve to meet the needs of learners. But we also iterated the approach to be more transparent and inclusive. We built upon the initial idea and invited teachers to submit requests for funding that aligned with our vision via email. These requests were coined "1-Sentence Grants" because they focused on student learning and were quick and easy to write. Making the process more open to everyone by pushing out the opportunity to submit a "1-Sentence Grant" brought more people in.[19] It also reduced the amount of red tape and work teachers needed to do in order to get support for the things they believed would make a difference. (Reducing the barriers and time sucks they encountered was also a small way to maximize their prep and family time.)

We did our best to support a variety of ideas and encouraged everyone to be mindful that we would not be able to honor all requests due to budget constraints. However, we were able to partially fund many of the larger requests so that teachers could move forward using other creative means.

Here are just a few examples of things that were funded through "1-Sentence Grants" that first year:

- $370 to replenish and build upon our existing fleet of Mobile MakerSpaces
- $500 to support more flexible seating options for students
- $282 to invest in photography equipment for a student club
- $100 to purchase a book series supporting character education
- $500 as seed money for a multisensory, brain-based room kindergarteners use

One of the unexpected benefits of this journey has been how our team encourages and empowers one another to consider positive changes and new perspectives. They often share insights on improvements that cost no money at all. For example, we received a suggestion to reconfigure how some book shelving was being used to better support guided reading in kindergarten. We also received a request to retrofit new table legs onto some old tabletops that were sitting in storage. This retrofitting transformed the tables into collaborative stand-up workstations for fifth graders. In both these examples, we supported staff members who were looking at using existing resources differently. Their capacity to innovate through resource maximization inspires me!

We monitor and adjust the budget each year so that we're able to provide a meaningful level of support. Therefore, we've needed to adjust the level of support to other projects depending on the value today's students and staff place on them.

Key Action Steps to Align Resources with Your Vision:

1. **Identify your priorities.** When we created our line item for "Innovation," we wanted to be more responsive to teachers' needs/ideas. We have tapped into this budget and the innovative grants we added more purposefully along the way. Random acts of maximization are less effective than intentional investments in meaningful work and people supporting

student learning. Having a shared vision and co-creating priorities is important.

2. **Be honest with yourself.** It wasn't until I started being honest with the fact our budget had remained relatively unchanged for a decade or more that I was able to own my role in the solution. Review your resources and reflect upon the degree to which they support the work students are most needing and motivated by. Ask yourself questions to push your reflection deeper: What evidence do you have to support the impact you think specific dollars are making? What might be the best thing that could happen if a change was made?

3. **Start small.** I don't recall the exact amount we dedicated to the line item for "Innovation" the first year we tried this approach. However, I know it was more about the mentality than the actual amount. Sometimes the best way to elevate something is to look for incremental wins. Momentum doesn't necessarily require additional dollars either! (What if everyone committed to finding the smallest possible thing that would improve your school . . . and what if you took these ideas and acted upon as many of them as possible? What would your school look and feel like after this process was established as part of the culture?)

4. **Don't stop.** The priorities our budget supports continue to evolve, as does our process. However, it is more nimble and aligned with our vision than it used to be. I'd go so far as to say the manner in which we strategically invest in classroom libraries for all grade levels barely resembles the first budget iteration we tried seven-plus years ago. But isn't this true of today's learners in some respects as well? The world is evolving. In order to maximize our impact, we need to keep our focus on the needs of those we serve. You can reveal what you're focused on by taking a long look at where your resources are

going. Keep reviewing. Keep learning. Don't stop looking for opportunities to grow.

As a principal, I'm always interested in strategies to implement ideas, to turn theory into action. One way to lead as a resource maximizer is to tap into the "First this, then that" protocol many of us use with students who are struggling with behavior. Typically, the "First this, then that" tool helps students understand and frame their schedules by placing a less-preferred task before a preferred activity or reward. But it also helps clarify what's actually needed/expected in a given situation.

Here's how you can apply a similar structure to elevate your impact and maximize what you do have when tackling an issue involving resource scarcity. For me, the temptation is always to compare or wish I had more staffing, more time, or a more robust budget. This simple protocol helps me develop the mindset needed to elevate my own thinking (while also creating the conditions for solution seeking in others).

Resource Maximizer "First this, then that" Protocol:

- FIRST, list the resources you do have. Your list doesn't need to be fancy, but be sure to think about the pockets of time that may be in the schedule. Also think about the dollars/people you're already investing in, as well as any flexibility you might have (aka the ability to adapt, adjust, or innovate within the constraints you're up against).
- Resist the temptation to compare your school to other schools, teams, or principals. Sometimes, we can look to others to glean inspiration (or cite precedence). But too often, comparing gets us stuck in a deficit mindset that sucks the solution-seeking oxygen out of a space.

- THEN, with a clearer understanding of the resources you do have, evaluate where they can be maximized. This doesn't mean you need to turn your current approach or budget upside down. Sometimes the smallest shift in resources/flexibility can ignite positive momentum and snowball into an unexpected impact in other areas. This is especially true when leaders make this type of thinking visible to others, involve them in the process, and link changes to shared priorities.

3 QUESTIONS FOR CONVERSATION AND REFLECTION

1 How might we move from the mindset of resource allocator to a posture of resource maximizer?

2 What is the first small step you can take to better align your vision with the resources you control?

3 How will you ensure your approach amplifies student and teacher voices in a meaningful way?

CHAPTER 15

Tapping into Our Most Influential Resource, the Teachers

BY SHANE SAEED

Instead of saying "I don't have time," try saying "It's not a priority" and see how that feels.

—LAURA VANDERKAM

I don't know how you do all the things you do!" I hear this a lot from family, friends, and colleagues who seem shocked by what is on my plate. I am always game to support an idea that could positively impact students and educators. Where there are fantastic opportunities to impact change, there must also be a structure to help make it happen. In order to make time for the projects I feel passionate about, I always look first to maximizing my resources: time and energy.

I have three specific habits that allow me to maximize my time and energy throughout the week. First, I plan all my outfits for the work week on Sunday based on the weather and events on my schedule. This buys me back the time I was using to plan outfits each night and is one less decision I have to make on a daily basis, as educators are notorious for decision fatigue. Second, on Sundays I also meal prep my breakfast and lunches for the week ahead in order to gain back the time I was using to pack a lunch each night. Bonus: I'm not spending extra money on eating out! Third, at the beginning of each workday, I take a look at my running to-do list housed on Google Keep and write a daily sticky note checklist where I prioritize the items I need to finish. When I take the time to prioritize, I find my time and energy goes toward the tasks that must get done rather than the tasks that may seem easy to accomplish but are not pertinent. All that to say, I am a fairly structured gal who thrives by maximizing her resources—so it is no shock that I admire the leadership of many of the principals who do the same.

As a district instructional coach, I serve multiple schools in my district. I have the luxury of seeing how different school systems ebb and flow. In my experience, school leaders who maximize their resources are able to create school systems that are both effective and sustainable—two components that produce positive long-term change. As discussed earlier in this section, the most expensive resource districts invest in are the staff members. By investing in them and supporting their growth, leaders are able to capitalize on everything they bring to the table as knowledgeable professionals. We know that, according to research, collective teacher efficacy has a substantial influence on student achievement. The best thing leaders can do is cultivate an environment where teachers are able to collaborate and support one another in their practice to positively impact their students.

One of the schools I have supported for the past three years has a leadership team of two incredible resource maximizers who also happen to be in the same doctoral program as me. As part of our doctoral coursework, we were tasked with writing a literature review around topics in education we are highly interested in that would later turn into our doctoral research projects. Jen, the dean of students, decided to research multi-tiered systems of support (MTSS) while Amber, the principal, researched evidence-aligned literacy practices. A MTSS system supports the needs of all learners by providing a foundational curriculum and the support to intervene with student learning or extend student learning when necessary. It was their collective vision to build and implement an MTSS process that empowered every teacher in the building.

As Jen researched MTSS processes that showed positive growth, she tapped into our district MTSS coordinator to hear about what had been working well in other schools. Through this connection, Jen learned the school district had been approved for a five-year grant from the state department of education to improve MTSS systems. Their school was invited to be a part of the training and work happening with the grant to improve their MTSS process.

Now that they were committed to overhauling their MTSS process, Amber and Jen reflected on the fact that having an MTSS subcommittee where only a sample of the staff was involved was not working. Amber had a vision to welcome the entire staff onto the MTSS team and work as a whole through the MTSS process. As their excitement built, they resisted the urge to make big decisions for the staff. Instead, they leaned into their staff and asked for their feedback on how to improve the process. Through individual teacher touchpoints, surveys, and ideas from teachers on the leadership team, they were able to start making incremental changes.

They realized they still needed a core MTSS mini-team where there was representation from the majority of the grade levels, special education, and counseling. The decision was made to keep this core team as case managers who would support the staff on a one-to-one basis when getting ready to present students to the whole staff team and checking in on how interventions were going after the six-week cycle.

Knowing their staff was the greatest resource they had, Amber and Jen decided to use one of the two staff meetings a month for MTSS. They changed the structure of the MTSS meeting to ensure everything ran in a timely manner. Each meeting starts with celebrations and then moves into a professional learning opportunity. This learning opportunity might be presented by the administration, special educators, or district personnel and targets a need or questions uncovered by the staff from prior meetings. Next, teachers introduce data about students they are concerned about using structured problem-solving protocols. Prior to the meeting, the teacher meets with their case manager to gather the appropriate data to present. Finally, the staff completes an anonymous feedback survey at the end of each meeting to glean what was working and what areas still need improvement. The feedback survey consists of a Likert scale (1–5) of how useful the teacher felt the meeting was and open-ended responses for what went well and what growth opportunities are available.

I will never forget the glee Amber and Jen had going through their feedback after the first whole-staff MTSS meeting. As they sifted through the responses, there were mainly threes, fours, and fives, but their smiles grew when they came across their first two. At first, I was confused. Why would they be excited for a low rating? Jen explained it was a celebration because the teacher felt safe enough to give honest feedback. They noted they cannot fix what they do not know is broken. Additionally, it was constructive feedback they would be able to bring to the MTSS mini-team to problem-solve.

Although they are still improving their MTSS process, the district MTSS team as well as leaders from other schools have come to Jen and Amber's school to observe their process as it continues to morph into an effective system. Teachers in their building have reported feeling more efficacious in sharing their instructional practices with their colleagues, receiving feedback, and making changes to increase student outcomes. Additionally, many teachers have written in their meeting feedback that even when they are not the one presenting a student, they leave those meetings with multiple ideas from colleagues they can bring back and use in their own classrooms to further support their students. Over the last two years, this collective teacher efficacy and collaboration has led to two-thirds of students on district reading plans for significant reading deficits being taken off as they are able to read on grade level.

So how did we get there? The first step is the mindset of the leader in knowing sustainable change is a marathon, not a sprint. For a task this large, it's important to think long-term and have a multiyear roll-out plan with milestones to celebrate along the way, as well as large year-end goals to direct your work. The MTSS changes Jen and Amber made were rolled out over several years.

Sustainable change is a marathon, not a sprint.

Second, cultivating an environment where teachers want to engage in this work is essential. Teachers are our greatest resource in education, and having consistency of instruction and care within a school is key. Jen and Amber's focus on maintaining a school culture aimed at retaining the teachers in their building allowed them to build on the momentum gained from the year before rather than having to start over each year with new employees.

Third, leaders can lean into invitational leadership and invite staff members to join the journey rather than force the journey upon them. By having individual and team conversations, leaders are able to plant seeds of change with a staff. This invites them into the work and onboards them as collaborative team members. Once a leader has their team on board, they can look into what resources are readily available within their network, like when Jen tapped into the district MTSS coordinator and learned about the grant work being done.

When the foundational pieces such as the plan, staff mindset, and ideas for outside building resources are set, a leader can focus on the structural factors that support the work. Jen and Amber live by the words of Marzano PLC trainer Kenneth C. Williams: "Do your minutes match your mission?" Jen worked hard to overhaul their master schedule to include dedicated data meeting time for teachers during their contractual day in order to have team-based discussions on student behavior and achievement, on top of the MTSS whole-team meeting. By reallocating meeting time to onboard the entire staff onto the MTSS team, they were able to use their time in a meaningful manner for all. These meetings continue to build collective teacher efficacy and tap into our most powerful resource in education, the teachers.

3 QUESTIONS FOR CONVERSATION AND REFLECTION

1 Do your meeting minutes match your mission? If yes, what celebrations can you bring back to your staff about that? If no, what might your first action step be for improvement?

2 What school initiative were you thinking of as you read Shane's story? What idea do you want to explore more?

3 How do you use teacher feedback for improvement, and how might you celebrate authentic feedback, even when it may be critical?

CHAPTER 16

Don't Wait for an Emergency

BY MIKE KLEBA

It's not the plane. It's the pilot.

—CHUCK YEAGER

When I was a new teacher, one of the healthiest things I did for myself was to occasionally blow off grading papers, microwave some popcorn, and sink into my couch (okay, it was a futon) to watch TV. My therapy was a show called *ER*. I have no idea if this show from the nineties still holds up, but I loved its look at the lives of the overworked doctors, nurses, and other hospital staff. And one of the best things I took away from my guilty pleasure was a new word, *triage*.

Triage is the emergency methodology used when the hospital was overwhelmed with patients. The staff, dealing with shortages, must make hard decisions about who gets treated and how they get treated. We could call triage a kind of resource maximizer leadership. The key question: How do I make the most of what I have?

I've had some great school leaders in my career. What I continue to learn in education, over and over again, is that the person doing the job is way more important than the title of the job. Not all principals, superintendents, or teachers are the same. Some leaders need things to go south before they maximize resources. The most effective ones don't need an emergency to become efficient.

It's in the Way That You Use It

In this chapter, we will meet two amazing school leaders and learn four action steps that a good principal can take to become a powerful resource maximizer:

1. Do your homework.
2. Change the game.
3. Believe in your team.
4. Build bridges.

The point is, it's not what you have when you lead at school. It's what you do with what you have. It's not the plane. It's the pilot.

Story #1: "The Details Matter"

Who your teacher is matters, and this is no less true in third grade than in grad school. While all of my professors at the Center for Integrated Teacher Education at the College of Saint Rose were hard workers, no one brought the thunder louder than my school finance instructor, Dr. Monica George-Fields.

Talk about impressive: Dr. George-Fields was the architect of New York State's Diagnostic Tool for School and District Effectiveness, a school and district review tool used to evaluate the practices of all federally identified schools and districts in the entire state. She'd worked closely with Dr. John King, United States secretary of education during the Obama administration, as well as the New York State Board of Regents, the New York secretary of education, and a number of NYC mayors. Along the way, she'd had nearly every leadership job possible in New York City's department of education, from principal to executive superintendent.

Dr. George-Fields was downright intimidating as a professor. And you know what she gave her students the hardest time about? The APA format of our papers.

"The details matter," she said matter-of-factly, probably a hundred times.

Do Your Homework

For Dr. Monica (which was the name she preferred us to call her in class), looking carefully at specifics wasn't simply a matter of getting things right. No, looking at specifics—"doing your homework," she would say—was about preparation.

"You need to know *what's on the paper*," she would say with the authority of a preacher. "People don't know what they have. It's criminal. You need to know the teacher's contract. You need to know *your* contract. You need to know the budget. *All* of the budget. The budget for salaries, for curriculum, for technology, for lunch, for transportation, for safety, for how much you're spending per football uniform. Up and down, backward and forward, all of it. *You need to be an expert on it.*"

Knowing these details allows you to find things when you need them, she told us. And it was just a matter of time until you would need them. Dr. Monica was a dead to rights resource maximizer. Looking at us coolly over her glasses, she deadpanned, "You are going to need to pay for things, and you are not going to have the money. What are you going to do then? I'll tell you. Look at *what's on the paper*." For Dr. Monica, school leaders who did not know the many opportunities to find money in their own budgets were committing malpractice.

And that wasn't Dr. Monica's only move.

Change the Game

"When you've looked over everything and you *still* can't find the money, you know what you do then?" We didn't.

"You go and *find the money*. You're a principal. You run a school. You're famous in your neighborhood. Get that fame to work. Go find partners. Go find supporters. Go find people who can start a booster club or a foundation. Change the game!"

That's exactly what Dr. Monica did. When she was an NYC principal of a low-scoring school, she reached out to her community to help underwrite programs for her school. She didn't simply enlist faculty members, parents, and local business owners. She looked beyond her school community and reached out to the CEO of JetBlue, David Barger.

"I called up the CEO. And he picked up."

A principal of a little school in Harlem got a globally known, billion-dollar company to pay for everything from field trips for her students to PD for her teachers. Dr. Monica and Barger worked together for six years, reducing teacher attrition and improving student outcomes. *Forbes* wrote about it.

"How did I do it?" she asked us. "I didn't wait for permission. I just did it."

When Dr. Monica couldn't find resources in the school, she maximized her resources by going outside her school. She rewrote the rules.

Dr. Monica's Action Steps on How to Be a Resource Maximizer:

1. Do your homework. Study your contracts and budgets like a lawyer.
2. Change the game. Use your imagination, be daring, and don't be afraid to ask for help from anyone who might help your school.

Story #2: We'll Do It Live

Before *The Addams Family* became a beloved TV show and blockbuster movie franchise, it was a cartoon, first published in the *New Yorker* magazine in 1938. The humor is oddball but playful, poking fun at suburban life using a kooky family that has delighted audiences for years. A few years ago, they made a Broadway musical of it.

In the second year of the pandemic, drawn to *The Addams Family's* story of redemption during a dark time, the team of teachers in our high school theatre department thought it would be a great musical to choose. As the director of the piece, I knew we had our work cut out for us. While high school theater programs across the country were opting to perform the shows over Zoom or Google Meet, we wanted to do it as a live, staged show with dancing and ensemble singing. We wanted the kids to do what live theater offers to students: high-stakes responsibilities, collaborative work, creative challenges, and the fun of expressing themselves.

The problem? We had no idea if we could actually do it.

Believe in Your Team

Enter from stage left: our new high school principal, Eric Contreras. A new transfer from one of the best schools in New York City, the famous Stuyvesant High School, he certainly had experience. But it was his first year with us, and he had a plate as full as a first go at an all-you-can-eat buffet.

We went to him to see if we could get permission. We also hoped for advice and help. And what did Mr. Contreras do? He paid attention to us. He didn't wonder why we picked the show. He didn't ask us to justify why we wanted to do a live-streamed staged performance (which, again, almost no one was doing anywhere). When he looked at us, he saw the passion and commitment this group of teachers had. And he turned all of us into a "we."

"What do we need?" he asked. "If we need it, we'll find a way."

Mr. Contreras was instrumental in creating a culture of possibility. It wasn't merely about him finding money, granting access to the theater, or offering up technological tools. It was about his unwavering belief in us, allowing students to be excused from classes to work on the production, ensuring they had a structured plan to make up their academic work, and facilitating crucial access to our tech department. He helped us teachers with subs—he personally covered some of my classes. Because he listened to us, we all worked harder and smarter.

The resource he maximized was us, his teachers and students.

Build Bridges

The PA announcements put smiles on our faces.

"Congrats to the amazing teachers in the theater program and their hardworking and talented students on another great week of rehearsal. I got a chance to witness them again this weekend, and I have to tell you, they need your help." Mr. Contreras's voice echoed through the hallways. "They are masters of collaboration in the theater, from students to adults. Kudos!"

"Who is this new principal?" students asked me and my fellow teacher. "He's really cool."

> **Resourceful leaders recognize that sometimes the greatest resource you can provide is your presence: showing up, advocating, and building relationships.**

He played diplomat to teachers in other departments, he rallied support from administrators, and he got on the phone to charm the parents. In the halls, he bumped elbows with freshmen and seniors. By actively participating in these interactions, he ensured everyone was on board, not just compliant. He removed barriers just by being present, acknowledging efforts, foreseeing issues, and acting before problems escalated.

Mr. Contreras's leadership reaffirmed that resource maximization isn't a stationary skill but a dynamic capability. It adapts, evolves, and, most crucially, empathizes. Resourceful leaders recognize that sometimes the greatest resource you can provide is your presence: showing up, advocating, and building relationships.

By the way, the show was an absolute smash. Our team trained our students for weeks, and the kids ran the whole thing, from cameras to mics to lights to the live stream. And Mr. Contreras was the first to congratulate us.

Mr. Contreras's Tips for Becoming a Resource Maximizer:

1. Believe in your team. Listen to your teachers and students. Their insights will help you maximize their strengths.
2. Build bridges and dismantle obstacles. Forge and nurture connections within and beyond the school walls.

3 QUESTIONS FOR CONVERSATION AND REFLECTION

1. Schools are overwhelmed with student needs. How will you use the triage analogy to determine the best course of action when maximizing resources?
2. Which of Mike's four action steps will you adopt?
3. What in the story about Dr. Monica resonated with you? How might you apply her lessons to your own leadership?

PILLAR FIVE
Visionary

Visionary leaders see into the future without losing sight of the present. They see what is possible for their community and create the path forward. They must be excellent communicators so they can lead others in creating a shared vision. Vision is just dreaming when it is not accompanied by action. Leaders must be action-oriented to be able to lead their team in taking the necessary steps to make the vision come to life.

PREFACE
Future Goes Last

BY GEORGE COUROS

Always do your best. What you plant now, you will harvest later.

—OG MANDINO

As Allyson and I planned this book, we decided that "Visionary" would be the last pillar we would share with great intentionality. Although it is extremely important in the leadership of a great principal, it is hard to create a compelling vision for your community when you do not know who you serve and what talents you have to build on. It is also essential to understand that the "vision" of a school community is not something for a principal to do in isolation, but something they must build together with their staff, as a community. We are more likely to realize our vision when we create it with other people.

In my first years of teaching, I thought the best teachers came into school a few weeks early, did all of their photocopying for the year, and could tell their leaders where exactly the class would be in the math curriculum on, say, November 18, at 9:30 a.m. I thought the best teachers would get students to where they wanted them to be, regardless of whether they wanted to go there or not.

As I grew as a teacher, I realized that if you are able to do that, it is more about you (or the curriculum pacing) than the students in your classroom. A teacher saying, "I need to get through the curriculum, and this is the timeline we need to be on," is a statement more focused on what the teacher is doing, rather than what the students have learned at any point in time. The time needed to teach a curriculum is usually different than the time needed for students to learn it. You might have taught the curriculum, but it doesn't mean anyone has learned it. It is essential for a teacher to know the people they serve before moving ahead, and it is no different for a great principal.

My high school football coach said something to me when I wanted to be captain that has stuck with me for years and applies here: **"You can be ready to lead all you want, but it only matters if people are ready to follow you."** That is why creating a vision together with your community is so necessary.

Building on Strengths to Create a Better Future

One of the things I am guilty of in my own practice is using the term *traditional teachers* with a negative connotation. I explicitly put quotation marks around that term and, if you can imagine, would say it like Dr. Evil from the Austin Powers movies, when I wanted to focus on bad practice. I have come to recognize that traditional does not equal bad, in the same way that new doesn't equal good.

Here is an example: we have focused on storytelling to bring our points to life throughout the book, and it is literally the oldest teaching practice in the world. Is it bad today? I don't think so. But how we tell stories has evolved. We can do it in a book, but you can also do it on a podcast, in a video, or even using pictures, without any words at all. That is why we say "A picture is worth a thousand words," which is truer today with the virality of internet memes. Although the delivery might look different as the world evolves, the basis of the practice is still very traditional.

I share this with you in a section focused on being a visionary because being visionary is not always about what is new, it is about understanding the context in which you lead, understanding the aspirations of your community, and co-creating a shared vision to move forward. In our modern world, a principal should understand what has worked and build on effective practices, but they also need to ensure that the school meets the needs of students today and guides them to their future, not our past. A visionary principal does not simply preserve the status quo; they communicate what is possible to create the best possible school for the community they serve.

What Impact Will Today Have Ten Years from Now?

So many schools focus on ten-year plans or being "future ready," but the way to deal with the future is by learning to adapt, and even creating it for yourself. You can ask your school community, "What do we want school to look like ten years from now?" and I think that is a very important question to consider. But a question of even greater importance is, "What are we doing in our classrooms today, and how will that enable our students and ourselves to be able to adapt and learn ten years from now?" Being "future ready" is not about a new pedagogy, technology, or trend, but about having a vision of empowering learners to adapt to change and navigate the path they choose.

As the quote widely attributed to Alan Kay states, "The best way to predict the future is to invent it."

Our vision starts with who we are and what we aspire to create for tomorrow.

Moving Forward

As shared at the beginning of this chapter, being a visionary doesn't necessarily come last in our leadership. In fact, none of the five pillars can be considered checkboxes, but areas of continued growth and development. But visionary definitely doesn't come first. You have to know your people, where they are, and where they want to go. This cannot be done by the principal alone.

And although we can work together to define *where* we want to go, we have to be open and allow people to get there in different ways and along different paths. In collaborating on this book, Allyson and I recognized that we have very different approaches to the writing process. This was important to us because we know that some readers will resonate more with her style than mine, and vice versa (or at least I hope vice versa). It was also essential to bring in other voices, not only so the reader could benefit from different perspectives but for us as authors to benefit as well.

Yet we shared a vision and had the same goal. It was to answer the question "What makes a great principal?" We have shared five pillars and provided diverse perspectives and experiences. We know that everyone reading this book will take something different for their own learning based on what they know, what they need, and where they want to go.

Perhaps being a visionary in your school community starts with a similar question: "What makes a great school?"

How you answer that question together, honor the past and present, and equip people to thrive in the future will help bring that vision together.

As the popular saying goes, "If you want to go fast, go alone; if you want to go far, go together." That is the best way to create a vision you'll be able to achieve—together.

CHAPTER 17

Visionary

BY ALLYSON APSEY

Great leaders are almost always great simplifiers, who can cut through argument, debate, and doubt to offer a solution everybody can understand.

—GENERAL COLIN POWELL

I am not a thrill seeker, but I was invited on a hot air balloon ride a few years ago by my superintendent at the time, and I nervously agreed. I mean, who could say no to an offer like that? It was a ride across the Grand Traverse Bay area in beautiful northern Michigan, and I was astonished at how peaceful it was. One amazing thing with hot air balloons is that when the conditions are just right, they can hover over a certain spot, and it is incredible to be able to identify details from that unique angle. I could see my house, the school where we worked, my grocery store, and the beautiful water and rolling hills off in the distance.

One way to tap into being a visionary leader is to pause and take a hot air balloon ride and hover over the current problem or situation to see it in its entirety. Pausing and hovering allows you to focus on how the components of the system are working together. I am preaching to the choir when I point out that principals deal with many day-to-day details that make it challenging to look at the big picture, but the reality is that if the principal does not pause and ascend in the hot air balloon, no one will. When principals take the opportunity to look at the broad view, they can identify where the current course of action is leading and the barriers that are getting in the way of progress, and know when to change direction.

The leader I took that hot air balloon ride with was the most visionary leader I have ever worked with, and her name is Kaye Mentley. She was my superintendent early in my administrative career, and I remember being amazed at how she could cut through the core of any issue with a laser-like focus on the possible solutions. She epitomized the idea of seeing the world differently, and General Colin Powell might have been describing her in the epigraph of this chapter. Her vision became an action plan, and she was very effective at getting others to share her vision and join in the action plan.

We worked together at a school that did not have bus transportation, which meant that massive lines of cars filled the parking lot and spilled into the street at dismissal time, bringing traffic in the surrounding area to a standstill. As we hustled to put students in the right cars as quickly as possible to move the line along, she walked around the building, thinking about how we could redesign the process. We were focused on the trees, while she took a look at the forest. None of us even thought about moving the entire operation to the other side of the school, but it worked like a charm and fixed the majority of the issues we were facing.

A few years after my first hot air balloon ride, I was able to attend the famous Balloon Fiesta in Albuquerque, New Mexico. Along with a couple close friends, I witnessed over six hundred hot air balloons ascend in quick succession, and the beauty was unbelievable. The conditions were perfect, and the horizon was full of balloons hovering around the area. Imagine if a school was full of staff members who ascend and dream together, just like those balloons. Not only will principals be able to solve problems if they schedule time for an imaginary hot air balloon ride, research finds that visionary leaders create visionary leaders.[20] The idiom "What is good for the goose is good for the gander" directly applies here. When leaders dream of the possibilities and then do the work to communicate effectively to make the dreams become reality, teachers feel permission to be dreamers also.

> **When leaders dream of the possibilities and then do the work to communicate effectively to make the dreams become reality, teachers feel permission to be dreamers also.**

Get to the Root

Visionary leaders know that the problem we see at the surface may not reveal the underlying root of the problem. As a principal, I have been guilty of jumping right into problem-solving mode without getting to the root of the problem. One specific example of this was when a teacher came to me with a scheduling issue. The teacher said he was talking with his team, and they identified that if their WIN (What I Need) intervention time was switched, it could maximize their ELA instruction time. Another teacher from the team of four also approached me about the same problem. So, being the efficient leader I am, I looked at the schedule and identified a change I thought solved the problem and then communicated the change to the four teachers and all other staff who would be affected.

Not surprisingly, after making the change, I found out that not all four teachers wanted the change to begin with, that the change caused additional issues in the schedule, and the other affected staff were not happy with the change. Whoops. Now I needed to backtrack and reverse the change after causing all the confusion and upset. Had I communicated with everyone who would be impacted as I was gathering information about the problem, I would have gotten to the root of the problem and solved the correct problem in a way that made sense to everyone involved. This could have been in the form of a quick stand-up meeting to get their input, or even a brief email asking for their thoughts.

Every single time I acted too fast or did not get enough input, I solved the wrong problem. In the situation I described above, the WIN intervention time was not really the issue; it was that students were hungry, and the teachers could not figure out how to fit snack time into their current schedule. Well, that is a totally different problem than the one I was solving. In order to think innovatively and to vision the future possibilities as a leader, it is important to get to the root of the problem first to make sure you are solving the right problem.

Schedule Crystal Ball Meetings

One of the most important things for school or district leaders to do is to schedule "Crystal Ball Meetings" for themselves. Those who consider themselves fortune-tellers may use a crystal ball to see into the future, and sometimes the visions foretell success and fortune, and other times the visions foretell really bad news. Using this concept with visionary leadership is helpful because there are two purposes to these meetings: to look into the future to see the possibilities, and to see what might happen if no change takes place. With this process, leaders can create a catalyst for action because they're able to envision the negative results of inaction. And they can envision the future by foreseeing the possibilities. Even taking just thirty minutes a week to look three and six months into the future can make a big difference.

A district I worked in started having Crystal Ball Meetings with community members by hosting the administration team meetings at local businesses. We would start our meeting with a tour of the business to hear their celebrations and their needs. We would talk with them about how the school system could serve their organization and the community as a whole better. We dreamed together and developed partnerships that led to improved programming and outcomes for students.

Once principals become effective and efficient during their own Crystal Ball Meetings, they can start scheduling them with staff members to guide them to do the same envisioning of the future. Here are some questions and talking points for these meetings:

- What are the two biggest challenges impeding the success of your students?
- Which challenge should we focus on first?
- Let's look three (or six) months into the future with that challenge. What might happen if nothing changes?
- If we were to resolve that challenge, what would success look like in three (or six) months?
- Let's give ourselves permission to experiment with possible solutions. Some will work and some won't, and that is okay.
- What is the first step you need to take, and how can I support you?
- Let's break down the action plan into a timeline to ensure success.
- What resources will you need in order to maintain the timeline?

As Crystal Ball Meetings become a part of your regular routine, principals can ask teachers to come to the meetings having already identified the two biggest challenges. Before you know it, teacher teams will have their own Crystal Ball Meetings and will start requesting meetings with you to dream together. As George mentioned in the introduction to the book, Todd Whitaker said, "When the principal sneezes, the whole school catches a cold." We can use that power for good because visionary leadership is contagious and can transform the culture of a school, and Crystal Ball Meetings are one way to make that happen.

The definition of a visionary includes words like *foresight, holistic, possibilities, imagination,* and *clear ideas.* There is one word that is often missing from those textbook definitions, however, and that is *dreamer.* When I think of visionary leaders, I think of this quote by Edmund Lee: "Surround yourself with the dreamers and the doers, the believers and thinkers, but most of all, surround yourself with those who see the greatness within you, even when you don't see it yourself." Visionary leaders see into the future without losing sight of the present, they see the world from a different angle than others, and they see paths forward that others miss. Like Lee said, they also see greatness in others that might be missed otherwise. Seeing beyond today into the possibilities of tomorrow is a crucial characteristic of a great principal.

The great news is that even though sometimes school leaders are born visionary and sometimes they are not, visionary leadership can be developed through purposeful strategies like the ones shared in this chapter. We can all be dreamers and doers, and we can create communities of dreamers and doers.

3 QUESTIONS FOR CONVERSATION AND REFLECTION

1 How are you a visionary leader, and what does that look like in daily practice at your school?

2 What strategy shared in this chapter would enhance your work as a visionary leader?

3 What gets in the way of spending time dreaming about three to six months in the future, and how might you overcome those barriers?

CHAPTER 18

People, Not Programs

BY LIZ GARDEN

People, not programs, change people.

—BRUCE D. PERRY

I remember when I was interviewing for an assistant principal position I was asked an interesting question, and I gave an honest, unconventional answer. The question I was asked was based on the fact that the teachers were using three different reading programs or curriculum. The interview team asked me how I was going to make that work. My honest answer? "I am not able to make that model work." The short answer was that if I was hired, I would help them go back to the drawing board and start over. It might have been a risky answer, but it was the truth, and my answer paid off because I was hired as the assistant principal. After two years in the role, I became the principal of the school.

That interview question wasn't a scenario or a hypothetical; it was their reality, and when I was hired, I was eager to jump in and help the school start over with the reading curriculum. I had the vision—I could see where we needed to go and what needed to be done to get us there. But I needed to make sure I wasn't the only one with the vision. I truly believe what George said about new leaders learning the strengths of all staff members before making any changes, and I knew that I had to develop relationships quickly, because some major changes needed to be made right away. We all needed to be united in our efforts.

There were a few things that I did right away to make sure the process was collaborative. First, we had a consultant come in, and alongside several teachers, we spent time observing what everyone was doing during our reading blocks. When we came together as a staff to discuss what was observed, the teachers who joined us on our learning walks were able to share our findings with their colleagues. Besides having teachers using all different programs, one unfortunate observation was that during the reading block kids weren't even reading. Our school had over five hundred students, and I think we saw three kids actually engaged with a text. We also saw students doing more worksheet activities and noticed there was less direct instruction foundational literacy skill development happening with teachers.

Sometimes as a visionary leader you need to take action and ask for forgiveness later. I did something a little radical at the beginning of this reading instruction overhaul. There were a lot of materials that came with one of the reading programs that had been piloted. The data was showing that the program wasn't working for our students, so I gathered up all of the materials and sold them to a company that bought used educational materials. I then used all of that money to revamp our classroom libraries. That was something else we noticed on our walkthroughs. Not only were kids not reading, many classrooms didn't even have books or libraries available. As a group, we decided on several nonnegotiables, including making sure that kids had more opportunities to actually practice reading, as well as access to more books throughout the whole school.

When I started to look at the data, it was definitely tough to digest. Our students receiving special education had made zero growth. Zero. Clearly something had to change. We also looked at our students who had been receiving reading intervention. The problem was they were receiving the same intervention year after year, and nothing was changing. I put everything up on the screen for us all to look at the data. The truth was, something had to change. The not-so-great data staring back at us was hard to look at, but it was also a tremendous motivator. Our kids deserved better. We needed to do better for them. I did not want to simply tell teachers what to do to change. They needed to be empowered to make changes, and once they saw the discouraging data, it was easy to get them fired up and ready for action.

Now that we were creating a vision for what needed to change, I had some ideas of what could help us move forward, but I wanted the ideas to come from the teachers. So I put them in a room, gave them time and some chart paper and whiteboards, and told them to come up with a plan. They came up with a small-scale version of co-teaching where special education teachers teach in the classrooms alongside general education teachers. It's amazing what can happen when leaders step aside, clear the obstacles, and get out of the way to let our educators chart new paths. That first year, the co-taught model, designed and implemented fully by the teachers, was a success.

We also sent some teachers on field trips to visit other schools that were utilizing a co-teaching model. We wanted to learn what was working and what might not work for us. The following year we expanded and created an entire co-taught classroom. The growth that we witnessed that year was astonishing.

> It's amazing what can happen when leaders step aside, clear the obstacles, and get out of the way to let our educators chart new paths.

In fact, at one point the special educator came to me with a problem: we were a third of the way through the year, and several students had already attained their benchmark goals. What a wonderful problem to have! We had to rewrite several goals that year. It was a welcome change from zero growth that had been happening before. While the academic progress was exciting, it was the response from the parents that was truly rewarding. Parents of children receiving specialized instruction were telling us that their kids loved school and that their kids were learning. That was the best feedback we could receive.

For the next several years, we continued to expand the co-taught model so that we had several grades co-teaching. We adjusted our reading intervention program so that students weren't spending year after year getting the same intervention and not making progress. We began to train educators in the principles of Universal Design for Learning (UDL). We made sure that general education teachers and special education teachers were communicating effectively with each other. Other schools started bringing their staff to observe what our educators were doing. Many of my teachers stepped out of their comfort zones and started presenting at conferences and workshops. After seven years of leading the educators in that school through lots of positive change, we found out that the school was being recognized as one of the top fifty schools in the state for high academic achievement, including elementary, middle, and high schools. To go from zero growth to top fifty in the state?! I would call that a win and one that was a direct result of a shared vision and then engaging and empowering educators to be change agents for kids.

So often as leaders we get bogged down in paperwork and policies, in programs and procedures, and at the end of the day, none of that matters if we are not doing everything we can for our people and with our people. Always remember that we are in the business of dealing with humans, big humans and little humans. And we are not unbreakable. But we are extremely capable of leading people, not programs, and transforming our schools. Visionary leaders can only be effective if the vision is shared and owned by all the stakeholders.

Action Steps for Leading People, Not Programs:

1. **Be brave.** I love wearing all kinds of different earrings, but my favorite pair has the phrase "Be Brave" on them in glittery cursive writing. It's a message that we all need to be reminded of on a daily basis, especially as leaders of change. Being a change agent and a visionary leader takes courage. Leaders need to be bold and honestly identify the issues in front of them. Too many times in education, we tiptoe around the problems, not wanting to upset people and not wanting to veer off the traditional path. But tiptoeing and path following won't bring about change. Leaders need to be brave and call it like they see it.

2. **Start from the beginning.** Sometimes we have to tear things down before we can build them up bigger and better. And that idea of starting over can be scary, which is why that brave piece in step one is so important. In the situation I described, the different curriculum resources being used weren't working, so we had to get rid of all of it and start over. Visionary leaders see where we all need to go, and they are not afraid to restart everyone on the path or even start over and forge a brand-new path.

3. **Clean up communication.** In my experience, 90 percent of problems arise as a result of poor communication, miscommunication, lack of communication, or one-way communication. As leaders, we need to make sure we are always clearly communicating our vision as well as our "why" behind all of our actions. We need to model proper communication so that educators will in turn communicate effectively with us and each other. We need to make sure we are giving and receiving

feedback effectively. We need to make sure we are hearing each other and actively listening.

4. **Be consistent with creative problem-solving.** Problem-solving as a school leader comes with the territory; it is the main part of our job description. But creative problem-solving is what moves people forward. We must think outside the box. We must not be afraid to push people to dream up creative solutions. However, we do need to remember the humans we are working with when we suggest a change or push the restart button. So many times we have great educators working so hard but not seeing the results. We need to make sure we depersonalize failure. I find that it is often not the people who are failing; it is the system that is failing them.

5. **Empower your people and look outside your bubble.** Amazing things happen when we put a group of dedicated educators in a space together and give them a blank slate. As visionary leaders, we need to know how to set up the right conditions for our educators to feel supported and empowered. As leaders, we can easily just tell people what to do, but everyone wins when we can empower our educators and distribute the leadership. You know you are in a groove when educators are coming up with new ideas, when educators are taking risks, when educators are stepping out of their comfort zones. Don't be afraid to visit other schools or meet with other leaders and educators. People are always willing to share, willing to collaborate, willing to tell you what they have learned during their transformative journeys. Take what works, leave what doesn't, and watch your educators mold their classrooms into something new and beautiful.

3 QUESTIONS FOR CONVERSATION AND REFLECTION

1   How would you have responded to the interview question that Liz was asked? Would your response be similar or different, and why?

2   Liz used data to influence her vision. How do you use data to determine your vision for your school? How do you communicate that with others?

3   Which of Liz's action steps do you want to implement or adapt right away? What is your first step?

CHAPTER 19

The Goldilocks Leader

BY DAVID DOMENA

Learn from yesterday. Live for today. Hope for tomorrow.

—ALBERT EINSTEIN

My stomach was churning. I reached a sweaty palm for the door handle to the meeting room and completely forgot to take the deep breath I had been saving all morning. This dreaded meeting with my principal and a parent of one of my students was sure to be uncomfortable, tense, and humbling—at best. At worst, it could mean disciplinary action. The only silver lining I had identified beforehand was knowing that, hopefully, we would all be on the same page in addressing the student's inappropriate and malicious behavior. He was extremely sneaky in provoking his classmates and then playing the victim if and when they retaliated.

As a new (second-year) teacher and having come to education as a second career, I was sure my time was up. My imposter syndrome raged as I greeted the parent and sat across from my principal, truly wishing I was anywhere else at that moment. What followed was an extraordinary master class by my principal on navigating parent deflection, concern, and bitterness. She did this without once throwing me under the proverbial bus or even acknowledging the parent's attempts to paint the picture that I disliked her student.

Leaving that meeting, I finally did take that deep breath; however, it was more a sigh of relief. I still couldn't shake the feeling that, any day now, SWAT team members would enter my classroom, shouting into their lapels, "Yep, he has no earthly idea what he's doing! He'll never teach again!"

Somehow, innately, my principal knew of my self-doubt. I vividly recall feigning confidence in her presence, the old, never-let-them-see-you-sweat fake out. However, as she visited my classroom that school year and we met for my formal observations, she got a glimpse of my solid teaching skills. She used these to bolster my confidence in my observation write-up, graciously stating, *Mr. Domena's students were consistently engaged in critical thinking and authentic learning experiences. Without even realizing it, Mr. Domena weaves high expectations throughout subject areas, lesson plans, and transitions.* She was exactly right: I hadn't realized that at all. Instead, I felt like my poor students had a lost year of instruction and may never catch up. She also expertly knew that if a beginning educator can gain, and maintain, student engagement, they are ahead of the curve and that curriculum, content, and standards can be learned.

Even several years later, I'll never forget her asking if I had ever read Dave Burgess's *Teach Like a Pirate*, a book that has since become a go-to resource. When I responded, "No, why?" she stated, "I feel like you wrote it." Curiosity sufficiently piqued, I ordered a copy and tore through it, floored not only at how I agreed with nearly every word but also by how my boss could ever consider me in the same educational universe. Little did I know that this book was part of Leslie's vision for student engagement at our school, and I was hooked!

These meaningful interactions allowed me to realize that Leslie Burghardt is the rare, exceptional leader who can build others up effortlessly. She exudes calm in the face of everything school leaders deal with on a daily basis from stakeholders: students (naturally), parents (whoa), teachers (gulp), and union personnel (yikes!). There were countless instances where the vibe of a meeting or event suddenly became much more secure by her mere presence. She manages to not only defuse a tense situation with an exceedingly even tone and demeanor but makes all involved feel as if they are the ones who should claim the credit.

Allyson used the term *Goldilocks* in reference to being a resource maximizer—that great principals match just the right resources with the needs, never too much and never too little. I think of Leslie as a Goldilocks leader because her effortlessly serene demeanor always feels "just right" in the myriad situations school leaders find themselves in daily. She strives to make all involved in a particular meeting or interaction feel comfortable with the outcome. Not everyone may feel thrilled with the outcome, but I cannot recall a time when I saw anyone leave more upset or frustrated than when they arrived.

I consider Leslie a visionary in terms of interpersonal communication. She is routinely empathetic to all involved in a situation, not only to those who can best serve her agenda. She considers future outcomes in regard to what is best for the greater good, even if that means altering her expectations in the process. Somehow, as a new administrator finding her way, she recognized that the quote George mentioned earlier holds true: "If you want to go fast, go alone, but if you want to go far, go together." She visualized where the school and its culture were headed, then held fast in her efforts to work as a team to get there.

Rooted Integrity

Leslie is not a complicated leader. She knows what matters to her most as a leader and reflects back upon what mattered to her most as a teacher and works tirelessly toward those few ideals. She was set on learning from what she saw in previous leaders, both what to emulate and what not to emulate, using that knowledge to be the best leader she can be today, and developing an actionable plan to make tomorrow as amazing as possible.

As an example, Leslie took over a campus in transition. Most of the staff were well-established veteran teachers, with a handful of new teachers (including me) finding their way. Without explicitly stating it, Leslie was clearly focused on being honest and transparent, in it for the kids, and learning right alongside her staff.

I remember a veteran teacher marveling at Leslie admitting a misstep and offering a sincere apology for it, something the veteran teacher hadn't experienced often in her career. This approach created trust with all staff, as Leslie exhibited the human side of being "the boss," rather than making herself the untouchable face of the school.

In my second year of teaching, I began to find my footing and educational style. I felt like I was getting this teaching thing down. So much so, I bristled at Leslie's urging toward the *Kids Deserve It!* movement sweeping the country, based on the book by Todd Nesloney and Adam Welcome, that challenged the status quo in education. It seemed hokey and cheesy to me, though I hadn't read a single page of it.

I swallowed my pride, trusting her twenty-five-plus years of experience as a visionary educational leader over my eighteen months' worth straight out of college, and jumped in alongside her. She began implementing ideas from the book, steadily moving away from the typical administrative response of "Why?" to most requests, and instead routinely asking, "Why not?"

This gradual approach was also refreshing and forward-thinking. More often than not, and seldom with much success, new leaders aim to make a splash with a significant change to the organization, in an attempt to justify their hiring. Leslie explicitly pushed against that faulty notion and focused instead on the long game of shifting the culture of the school and adopting a can-do outlook. She also knew when to cut someone loose on an idea or project and when to work alongside them each step of the way. Again: just right.

Challenge Embracer

> **Great principals make challenges seem surmountable.**

Great principals make challenges seem surmountable. There wasn't a time where Leslie threw in the towel or even hinted at that dreaded four-letter word, *can't*. This approach served her exceedingly well as she hand-delivered lunches to mobile homes and houses during the COVID-19 shutdown and implemented forward-thinking programs to make her school site a place students clamored to attend, increasing enrollment in her time as principal.

She also courageously sought out a positive relationship with the families of the toughest students on campus in an effort to understand the students more fully and decrease the number of poor choice instances. The valuable information she was able to gain was far more effective as she was coaching the student, as the student understood that Leslie knew the support system coming from the home environment. A quick "Hmm, I wonder what your football coach would think of this" or "Aunt Jenny is picking you up today, and I would love to give her a great report!" worked far more wonders than even the most forceful "Stop doing that!" ever could.

Staff members who had struggled with some of those same students in years prior watched in awe as Leslie was able to place them in leadership roles specifically tailored for their ages and personalities. These students took these roles extremely seriously, pridefully training other students before they themselves were promoted to middle school. Even better, a natural, built-in consequence emerged that they desperately wanted to avoid: losing their job. The mere mention of it would shape them up quickly if and when they found themselves straying from the leadership path.

Here Are Some Action Steps That Summarize Leslie's Visionary Leadership:

1. Identify the goal of an initiative and the key measures to get there. Trust yourself and don't stray from those.
2. Recognize team members who can and will do the work. Let them lead, and if necessary, push others to join the movement. Support them along the way with finances, resources, or a listening ear to avoid burnout.
3. Celebrate successes, both during and after. This will make the work feel meaningful, encourage others to join the next project, and increase the odds that the project leads to another success down the road.

3 QUESTIONS FOR CONVERSATION AND REFLECTION

1. We have heard stories about principals who lead with integrity, like Leslie. What does that mean to you as a current or aspiring leader, and how will your sense of integrity play out in your leadership?
2. Leslie turned a challenge into an opportunity by building connections with student families, especially those who were struggling with behavior expectations. What challenge could you turn into an opportunity?
3. In what way are you a "Goldilocks leader," where you focus on providing just the right amount of support or guidance—not too much and not too little?

CHAPTER 20

Being a Clear and Present Principal: Jonathan Dyal

BY VICKI A. DAVIS

Leaders who don't understand how to serve do not understand how to lead.

—PAT WILLIAMS

Knowing how to be a great principal is good; humility with that knowledge is great. Leading by example is good; leading by serving is great. Telling teachers the right thing to do in the classroom is good; modeling great teaching when you hold teacher professional development is great. Having effective staff meetings is good; knowing when to have a meeting and when to cancel or shorten the meeting is great.

Books have been written about "good to great," and sometimes the difference between good and great is subtle, but when you work for a truly great principal in a well-run great organization, you know it. Everyone does. In this chapter, I'm going to share five aspects of what it means to be a "clear and present principal" and how my secondary principal at Sherwood Christian Academy, Jonathan Dyal, exhibits these attributes.

Before school started this year, I knew something was different. I was surveyed and asked what I wanted to see for professional development. Wow. That was a first! Then, when school started, two things happened. First, I was observed. A lot. My new principal, Jonathan Dyal, was coming into my room constantly. But it wasn't like the fifty-minute-long observations I'd experienced before, where the principal comes in with a clipboard and pencil and is writing the whole time. He came in for fifteen minutes and then left. Then, I'd receive an email with an overview of what was observed. I'd never seen observations done like this before, and it was quite, well, refreshing!

To add to this, I had a student come in to class and ask if he could be excused for this one day. When I asked why, he said, "Principal Dyal is playing a pickup basketball game with us in the gym, and I want to play." Wow.

I say that Jonathan is clear and present because he is very direct and clear with us—about good and bad things happening—and he is also extremely present and around all the time. Each thing he does with us shows a clarity of purpose and focus. I've seen this happen in five ways: how he moves around the school, how he leads teacher PD, how he gives teacher feedback, how he provides teacher support, and how he started strong in a new job as principal to make an impact on day one.

Clear, Visible Presence around Campus

For teachers, routines are part of what we do every day. I get used to the movements of other teachers and administrators and know when to expect to see them around campus. However, while I see Jonathan at lunch almost every day, I notice that he seems to intentionally move around the campus differently from day to day.

In between classes one day, he goes one way, and another day, he literally goes another way. This gives the appearance of him being many places, just because you don't know when to expect his presence. It almost feels like he's always there. ELA teacher Dawne Beck told me that her students described Mr. Dyal as "omnipresent" and another said that he "teleports."

When I asked Jonathan about this practice, he said, "My approach is proactive rather than reactive. If I am present or thought to be present at any moment, students choose not to participate in inappropriate activities because they know I could be around at any time."

Jonathan extends this to activities students love. He's often seen playing pickup basketball in the gym during seventh period, or during Homecoming week, you'll see him move through the whole campus and speak to students individually. While they know he is an administrator with authority, they also know he is constantly present, and it does improve behavior and camaraderie among students and faculty.

Teacher PD That Clearly Models Excellent Teaching

Our teacher professional development is clearly a result of teacher choice (through a survey conducted weeks before PD) and intentionally designed to model excellent teaching. If Jonathan wants cooperative learning happening in the classroom, he uses cooperative learning in our PD session. If we want formative assessment used in the classroom, our PD uses formative assessment. Great principals model the vision they have for classroom instruction.

> **Great principals model the vision they have for classroom instruction.**

Jonathan says, "Choice is a major push in teaching students because it allows students a say in what they are learning or doing in the class. Teachers should be offered the same options. It also helps create buy-in in new initiatives."

The surveys Jonathan conducts aren't just wide open but intentionally designed. Before professional development happens, Jonathan sits down with administrators to clarify the vision for classroom teaching.

Next, he informally polls some teachers to collect more ideas and looks for patterns before creating his survey. Then, he crafts a Google Form to ask teachers which of the options would be best for everyone in order to create a personalized professional learning day that helps everyone. He also asks teachers which areas they believe they have expertise in to provide support to other teachers.

In addition to providing helpful PD that aligns with how I'm expected to teach in the classroom, Jonathan also attends the PD as a participant in the session. His presence shows the importance he places upon what we are doing to improve our skills, and because he is present, he is able to quickly clarify questions from teachers to help build momentum for initiatives.

Consistent Teacher Feedback

Furthermore, Jonathan extends his presence into the classroom. I never know when the doorknob will turn and he will come into my classroom to see what is happening. In fact, when this chapter emerged, I had just been observed for the eighth time that school year (it was still very early in the school year), and I tweeted about how much I loved that.

Missy Sanders, who teaches AP US history at our school, said she was talking with Jonathan once about an out-of-the-box idea and he immediately said, "That sounds fun. Let me know when you're doing it. I want to watch."

Sometimes when he's in the classroom, students will tell him about special projects they are doing in other classes, and he makes it a point to drop in to see their science project or history presentation.

After he observes my class, I receive a quick email rating me on the five things he's looking for in his informal observations, with a note on each. These five things weren't a surprise but were the subject of PD during preplanning, so we'd be ready for how we'd be evaluated this year.

Teacher Support

Jonathan is a listener and noticer. Sometimes getting teacher support is as small as "getting" what teachers really need to feel supported. Sometimes it is noticing that a teacher has something happening and needs to leave five minutes early. Other times it is realizing that teachers are in the midst of grading, and nothing is more important than completing that task, and so the staff meeting can wait.

> **Sometimes getting teacher support is as small as "getting" what teachers really need to feel supported.**

For me, it was a small comment after a particularly challenging parent-teacher conference. I'm a pleaser by nature, and there have been times I've had principals make me feel that my job was to please parents. In this case, the meeting ended amicably, and yet the parents and I agreed to disagree.

Jonathan picked up on my frustration. I felt I had let him down and the school down but knew that what I had shared was the truth, even if it wasn't accepted as such. He turned to me and said, "I have been in many challenging parent-teacher conferences. That is the best I've seen 'agreeing to disagree' handled. I think what was needed was communicated, and it went well, and I'm telling you I'm okay with it, so let's move on."

I drove home with a deep breath that night. Instead of replaying the conference in my mind, I let it go. I let it go because Jonathan was present with me in the parent-teacher conference, and he was clear with me after it was over about my performance. Even if he had told me I could have handled it better, knowing where you stand as a teacher gives teachers a solid foundation upon which to build excellence in the classroom.

Not Waiting to Get Started

I have had many world-class administrators and teach at an awesome school, but I have never seen someone make an impact as quickly as Jonathan Dyal. I asked him about his strategy for starting strong, as sometimes it is easy to think it will take a while to make an impact.

He said, "Starting new is a challenge, but finding the balance of where to sit back and listen and when to get started is necessary for success. There will be times where you should have acted and sat back, and there will be times when you should have listened and you acted, but being willing to find the balance will help you impact your work environment from day one. Don't always wait to be told what to do—just do it."

Being a Clear and Present Principal Makes a Clear Difference in My Classroom

Our headmaster, Kenny Roberts, says, "Mr. Dyal is consistent in class observations and student discipline," and this is true, but there is a certain unpredictability about his presence that improves student behavior and keeps all of us teachers excited to teach. We know he notices when we do extra and have an exciting lesson. It makes me even more excited to teach when I know he is paying attention to what is happening in my classroom.

I feel seen. My students feel seen. I have a clear and present principal who puts vision into action, and it shows.

3 QUESTIONS FOR CONVERSATION AND REFLECTION

1   How did Jonathan's intentionality impact how he was accepted as a new leader?

2   Vicki shared many things that Jonathan did to help teachers and students feel seen and valued. What idea did you take away from Vicki's story?

3   How do you hope teachers feel about classroom observations? What steps might you take to make observations a positive experience?

CONCLUSION
What Will Your Fingerprints Be?

BY GEORGE COUROS

When you work in hospitality—and I believe that whatever you do for a living, you can choose to be in the hospitality business—you have the privilege of joining people as they celebrate the most joyful moments in their lives and the chance to offer them a brief moment of consolation and relief in the midst of their most difficult ones. Most importantly, we have an opportunity—a responsibility—to make magic in a world that desperately needs more of it.

—WILL GUIDARA

What a blessing it is to be able to write the final chapter of this book after the amazing stories from people whose lives have been transformed by great principals. There is not much I can say after these stories, but I wanted to share one last call to action.

As Allyson and I discussed what this book could be, we wanted to ensure that it provided the perspectives of people who not only served or currently serve in the principal position, but people who have been impacted by principals. My immigrant parents owned a restaurant for the entirety of my childhood and school experience, and so much of what I learned about leadership was from watching them and hearing their advice. Working in hospitality, my parents taught me that the higher up you go in any organization, the more people you serve, not the other way around. Those words couldn't ring truer for a principal, and this idea is embodied in the stories in this book.

How Will People Know You Were Here?

When I was an assistant principal, I remember receiving an email from my superintendent, Mary Lynne Campbell, for an early morning meeting. I had a feeling that I was about to be assigned the role of a principal position, and I was both excited and nervous about the prospect. So nervous, in fact, that about fifteen minutes into my thirty-minute drive to her office that morning, I realized that I was wearing two different shoes, one brown and one black. Oh boy.

I walked into her office that morning and said, "Before you say anything, I want you to know that I do know I am wearing two different shoes, and I am not making a fashion statement or anything like that—I was just nervous about today! Please don't see this as how I would lead a building!" Talk about resource maximizer! My mentor, Kelly Wilkins, taught me the best way to deal with a mistake is to own it. Mary Lynne appreciated my candor and has mentioned that moment often. Sometimes our biggest embarrassments become our best memories.

As I had expected, she let me know that I would be assigned to a principalship, and I was busting out of my black and brown shoes with excitement. Then she said something to me that I will never forget: "George, the school had a great principal already, and much of her work will last during your time and after. You want to build on that. But I want you to really think about this question: What will your fingerprints be on this school? After you leave, how will people know you were there?"

Before I started, my exit was already being planned! Stupid shoes!

In all seriousness, those words have stuck with me long past the principalship, and I think about them often.

On my first day walking into this brand-new (to me) school that was probably seventy-five years old, I remember looking at everything with fresh eyes. How could I not? Everything was new to me, and I wanted to take it all in.

> **What will your fingerprints be on this school? After you leave, how will people know you were there?**

Whether you've just become a principal or you've been in that role for years, try looking at everything with fresh eyes; don't become numb to the little things in your school that might be old to you but new to people entering your building. Everything sends a message of who you are as a community, whether you pay attention or not.

To my right as I entered the main doors was the principal's office, and it was entirely made out of glass. Not only did I love the look, I loved the location. It was right at the front entrance, and I could see every person entering the building.

Then I noticed a gymnasium to my left, and above the gymnasium doors was a picture of every single principal who had ever served in that school. I watched students walk in every single day, and I never saw one of them look up at those pictures and say, "That was the principal in 1972? Amazing!"

Nobody cared.

The amazing thing I often hear from adults is how they say, "Kids these days are so narcissistic posting these selfies on Instagram," and all I can think when I hear that is that we used to post portraits of ourselves on walls! That's narcissism!

But I was new to the building, and I said nothing about it. I wanted to get to know the people I served, so I sat back and learned as much about the community as I could.

About two months in, the secretary said to me, "Hey, George, when are you getting your portrait for the wall?"

I replied, "Oh no, I am not getting my portrait for the wall."

She said, "Well, you have to—you are the principal!"

I laughed and said, "Actually, I don't! That is the beauty of my job. I am not going up on that wall!"

In the next staff meeting, I brought up the pictures. I shared with everyone that I noticed they believed the same thing I did—"We are all about kids!" But those portraits did not represent that. They sent the message that the most important person in the building was the principal, not the kids, and not even the staff as the community. Those portraits needed to be removed from the front foyer.

I was shocked by the initial response from my staff and the gasp I heard: "You can't take those pictures down! That is tradition!"

One of my favorite quotes ever, even though I have no idea where it came from: "Tradition is peer pressure from dead people."

It is a beautifully jolting statement.

Am I against tradition? Absolutely not.

In fact, to make my point, I often tell stories, and storytelling is one of the oldest teaching practices in human history.

If we do things in our schools and classrooms that were done hundreds of years ago that still work today, we should continue to do them. On the other hand, if we do new stuff just because it is new, but it doesn't work, we shouldn't be doing it. Whatever works for our community is where our focus should be, no matter when it originated.

What I am against is doing things just because we have always done them. That is my problem.

Eventually, I talked my staff out of those pictures, and we replaced them, and you all know with what—pictures of our students. We would replace them every two months or so, and I would watch students walk in every single day, look up, and say, "I am on the wall! I am on the wall!" I never saw the same enthusiasm for those principal pictures.

Once we saw that enthusiasm for students seeing themselves on the walls, we asked, "What happens when students see themselves in the books we read and the lessons we teach?" That subtle change on the walls changed a lot, not only about what the building looked like in our school, but most importantly what learning looked like. The pictures catalyzed rethinking and recommitting to the change we aspired to create when we first entered the profession.

So going back to Mary Lynne's question: "What will your fingerprints be on this school? After you leave, how will people know you were there?"

Well, if my portrait was up on that wall, it would be pretty easy for people to know I'd been there.

But do you know what I prefer? To this day, when you enter that building, you still see student pictures on that gymnasium wall. Most people have no idea that I had anything to do with it, and honestly, I don't care. I would rather have my legacy be that I changed things for the better in that school.

Yet what is on the wall is not as important as the fingerprints you leave on the hearts and minds of the people you serve in your role. Over and over again, it is confirmed that great principals help bring out gifts and talents in their staff and students that they might not have seen in themselves. That is why it was so important in this book to share those stories from people who have been impacted by great principals. The impact and legacy of those great principals will last long past their time in the role.

To end the book, I will ask you to consider the same question Mary Lynne asked me before I became a principal.

What will your fingerprints be on your school? After you leave, how will people know you were there?

Your legacy will become part of the legacy you inspire others to create for themselves.

ENDNOTES

1   Todd Whitaker, *What Great Principals Do Differently: Twenty Things That Matter Most*, 3rd ed. (New York: Routledge, 2020).

2   Douglas Reeves, *Fearless Schools: Building Trust, Resilience and Psychological Safety* (Massachusetts, Creative Leadership Press, 2021).

3   Gregory F. Branch, Eric A. Hanushek, and Steven G. Rivkin, "School Leaders Matter: Measuring the Impact of Effective Principals," *Education Next* 13, no. 1 (2013).

4   Sanée Bell, *Be Excellent on Purpose* (Highland Heights, OH: Times 10 Publications, 2019).

5   Paul Spiegelman, "Your Company Is Not a Family," *Harvard Business Review* (June 2014). Accessed February 27, 2024. https://hbr.org/2014/06/your-company-is-not-a-family.

6   Sharon K. Parker and Nancey Hoare, "The Value of Belonging at Work," *Harvard Business Review* (December 2019). Accessed October 18, 2023. https://hbr.org/2019/12/the-value-of-belonging-at-work.

7   R. Allan Allday and Kerri Pakurar, "Effects of Teacher Greetings on Student On-task Behavior," *Journal of Applied Behavior Analysis* (Summer 2007).

8   John Hattie, *Visible Learning: The Sequel* (New York: Routledge, 2023).

9   Arthur C. Brooks, *Build the Life You Want: The Art and Science of Getting Happier* (New York: Penguin, 2023).

10 Denzel Washington, *A Hand to Guide Me* (New York: Meredith Books, 2006).

11 The Wallace Foundation. "How Principals Affect Students and Schools: A Systematic Synthesis of Two Decades of Research." (October 2021). https://wallacefoundation.org/report/how-principals-affect-students-and-schools-systematic-synthesis-two-decades-research.

12 Rachel Eells, "Meta-Analysis of the Relationship Between Collective Teacher Efficacy and Student Achievement," ResearchGate (January 2011). https://www.researchgate.net/publication/254615557_Meta-Analysis_of_the_Relationship_Between_Collective_Teacher_Efficacy_and_Student_Achivement.

13 Solution Tree. "Solution Tree: Rick DuFour on Groups vs. Teams." YouTube, October 9, 2009, https://youtu.be/0hV65KIltlE?si=v142VwVvgU1OokjB.

14 Richard DuFour, Rebecca DuFour, Rober Eaker, Thomas Many, and Mike Mattos, *Learning by Doing: A Handbook for Professional Learning Communities at Work*, 3rd ed. (Bloomington, IN: Solution Tree Press, 2016).

15 Madeline Will, "Efforts to Toughen Teacher Evaluations Show No Positive Impact on Students," *Education Week* (November 29, 2021). https://www.edweek .org/teaching-learning/efforts-to-toughen-teacher-evaluations-show-no -positive-impact-on-students/2021/11.

16 Robert K. Greenleaf, *The Servant as Leader* (Robert K. Greenleaf Publishing Center, 1970).

17 Jessica Grossmeier et al., "Linking Workplace Health and Promotion Best Practices and Organizational Financial Performance," *Journal of Occupational and Environmental Medicine* 58 no. 1 (2016), 16–23.

18 Walter Isaacson, "The Real Leadership Lessons of Steve Jobs," *Harvard Business Review* (April 2012). https://hbr.org/2012/04/the-real-leadership-lessons-of -steve-jobs.

19 Brad Gustafson, "1 Sentence Grants." Brad Gustafson's blog (April 2, 2017). https://www.bradgustafson.com/single-post/ 2017/04/02/1-sentence-grants.

20 Mingwei Liu, Pengcheng Zhang, Yanghao Zhu, and Yang Li, "How and When Does Visionary Leadership Promote Followers' Taking Charge? The Roles of Inclusion of Leader in Self and Future Orientation," *Psychological Research and Behavior Management* 15 (2022): 1917–1929. doi: 10.2147/PRBM.S366939.

ACKNOWLEDGMENTS

From George:

I have been blessed to have amazing principals in my life and was inspired in particular by Kelly Wilkins, who saw something in me at a time when I wasn't able to see something in myself. This book, my career, and so many aspects of my life wouldn't be possible without her leadership.

Dr. Katie Martin is one of my most trusted partners, and I would not even consider publishing this book without her critical and thoughtful eye before sending it off for revisions. She has such an amazing pulse on what education can be and helps me clarify my thinking and writing in a way that no one else seems to do.

This book would not have happened if I hadn't been inspired by my co-author's writings and the wisdom she has shared in countless books. Although this idea was something we had been discussing for over a year, it was while reading her book *Leading the Whole Teacher* that I was inspired to find a vision for what this book could be to help others reach their full potential. Allyson is an inspiration in so many ways, and I could not be more proud to write this book with her. I am so proud that I wrote this with her, and I am even more proud of how good of friends we became throughout the process.

From Allyson:

Have you ever been to Bell's Brewery in Kalamazoo, Michigan? Well, I am not even sure we were drinking beer that night back in December 2015, but that is where the story of this book begins. Some might call it serendipity. It was on the eve of George Couros's keynote speech at the Michigan Elementary and Middle School Principals Association (MEMSPA) annual conference that our paths crossed. Between our brief chats that evening at the brewery and the insights shared during his keynote, my life underwent a significant transformation. Much like the countless others influenced by George's words, I found myself compelled to take action, and days later I started my blog, "Serendipity in Education." This initial step set in motion a journey that led to writing several books and the opportunity to travel the country, inspiring and being inspired by thousands of educators. This journey continues in the co-authorship of *What Makes a Great Principal* with George. He is a mentor, my biggest fan and worst critic, and, most importantly, a dear friend. My enduring gratitude extends to him for the profound impact he has had on the trajectory of my life.

ABOUT THE AUTHORS

George Couros

George Couros is a worldwide leader in the area of innovative teaching, learning, and leading, and has a focus on innovation as a human endeavor. Most importantly, he is a proud father to Marino, Georgia, and Kallea, and husband to Paige. His belief that meaningful change happens when you first connect to people's hearts is modeled in his writing and speaking. In his twenty-plus years in the field of education, he has worked at all levels of school, from K–12, as a teacher, technology facilitator, and school and district administrator, and is currently an adjunct instructor with the Graduate School of Education at the University of Pennsylvania. George is also the author of the books *The Innovator's Mindset: Empower Learning, Unleash Talent, and Lead a Culture of Creativity*; *Innovate Inside the Box*; *Because of a Teacher*; and *Because of a Teacher, Volume II*.

You can learn more about George at his website: georgecouros.com.

Allyson Apsey

Allyson Apsey has been an award-winning school leader for over twenty years, leading all levels, from elementary to high school. Her favorite role is mom to her sons, Laine and Tyson, and wife to Jim. She loves working with passionate groups of educators to support them in taking care of the whole child and the whole educator by implementing research-proven practices. Allyson's TEDx Talk can give you insight into her passion. She is a national keynote speaker and the author of several books, including the best-sellers *Lead with Collaboration*, *Leading the Whole Teacher*, and *The Path to Serendipity*. She also wrote the picture book *The Princes of Serendip*. She currently works as an associate for Creative Leadership Solutions, supporting schools and districts as a collaboration and leadership coach.

Connect with Allyson on social media (@AllysonApsey), and learn more about her at allysonapsey.com.

ABOUT THE CONTRIBUTORS

Dr. Marcus Belin is a principle-driven and passionate servant leader who is committed to the work as an educator and school leader. His goal is to create learning environments where students know they are, first and foremost, loved and cared for and to expose young people to the world around them through meaningful learning experiences. Dr. Belin currently serves on  the board of directors for the National Association of Secondary School Principals, and was the 2021–2022 president of the Illinois Principals Association, the 2021 Digital Principal of the Year, the ASCD Class of 2021 International Emerging Leader, and the 2020 Illinois High School Principal of the Year for Kishwaukee Region. Dr. Belin is a motivational speaker and podcast host of *Unapologetic Leadership*. You can connect with Dr. Belin on X (@marcusjbelin), Instagram (@drmarcusbelin), and through his website, drmarcusbelin.com.

Dr. Ryan Daniel currently serves as the principal of Fort Foote Elementary School located in Prince George's County Public Schools (PGCPS). Dr. Daniel displays a sincere dedication to serving as an innovative educational leader. Transforming learning environments for students to feel supported, seen, and valued is her mission as an educational leader. Dr. Daniel believes

in providing supportive environments for teachers to build and enhance their capacity through intentional coaching and empathetic leadership skills. Currently Dr. Daniel serves as the president for the Maryland Association of Elementary School Principals (MAESP) and a fellow for the National Association of Elementary School Principals (NAESP), leading the Center for Diversity in Leadership. Dr. Daniel has contributed to the book *She Leads: The Women's Guide to a Career in Educational Leadership*, which highlights the voices and stories of women educational leaders. Most recently Dr. Daniel has been named as the 2023 *Washington Post* Principal of the Year for Prince George's County Public Schools. You can connect with Dr. Daniel on X and Instagram (@HeyDrDaniel).

Vicki Davis is a twenty-two-year classroom teacher and Instructional Technology coach. She teaches AP Computer Science Principles, Digital Technology, and Computer Applications. Vicki blogs at the award-winning *Cool Cat Teacher* blog and hosts the *10 Minute Teacher* podcast. In addition to being named the Top Global Eduruptor for 2021, she won the ISTE Online Learning Award in 2006 and the top Podcast Host in Education BAMMY Award, but her greatest honor was being named Eric Bergrab's STAR teacher in 2022. You can connect with Vicki Davis on social media (@coolcatteacher) or through her website, coolcatteacher.com.

David Domena is an elementary educator passionate about creating meaningful and memorable learning experiences for students. He models making mistakes and a "know failure" rather than a "no failure" approach. He comes to education as a second career and recalls that his worst days in education are far better than 99 percent of his days in retail warehousing. David has taught second, third, and fourth

grades, and is now the STEAM teacher at an elementary school in Southern California, working with all 525+ K–5 students every week. He has implemented various school clubs, schoolwide house systems and art shows, and annual Amazing Shake competitions. He has coached countless students to find their voice through leadership roles around campus. David strives to maintain positive relationships with all students through high expectations, celebrating even the smallest successes and visibly shuddering at any mention of the word *can't*. You can connect with David on X and Instagram (@mrdelementary).

Dr. Emily Freeland has over thirty years of experience that includes administrative positions at the state, district, and school levels, as well as teaching science. Much of her work has been concentrated in schools that were identified as underperforming and targeted the implementation of school turnaround principles, the effective use of data, closing achievement gaps, and increasing graduation rates. She currently serves districts and schools across the nation as an instruction and leadership coach. Emily's book, *From Ghost to Graduates: An Educator's Guide to Identifying and Reconnecting Disengaged Students*, highlights her expertise as a certified National Dropout Prevention Specialist and focuses on strategies that address the causes of disengagement, including the context of pandemic learning and its impact on students who were previously not at risk of dropping out.

Liz Garden is the current principal of Henry P. Clough Elementary School and has been an educational leader for fifteen years in Massachusetts. Before becoming a school leader, Liz spent eleven years teaching students from preschool through high school. Liz serves as an editorial advisor for NAESP's *Principal* magazine. She was recently selected to serve as an NAESP fellow for the Center  for Innovative Leadership and works with school leaders across the country to highlight transformative and innovative practices that serve as catalysts for shaping the long-term impact of school improvement efforts. She has provided a voice for principals across Massachusetts as a member of DESE's Principal Advisory Cabinet and across the country as a member of the ASCA advisory board and NAESP's National Coronavirus Task Force. Liz served as the president of the MSAA in 2022 and is currently a leadership coach for MSAA. Liz was part of the team of literacy experts from across the state who advised DESE in the creation of the MASS Literacy Resource Site and was selected to be a member of the MASS Literacy Support Network. She was selected to serve on a national cadre for Reading Universe, charged with designing an online professional development site for literacy instruction. She also provides support to Bookelicious to help spread the joy of reading. She has presented at several national association conferences, including NAESP and NASSP, and has presented professional development locally to educators and school leaders at events hosted by MSAA, MassCUE, Codebreaker, MRA, and Literacy for All, usually around the topics of literacy, innovative leadership, and Universal Design for Learning. Liz is a student-centered leader who believes all kids are our kids. She enjoys working with educators and leaders to help them be the best they can be for kids.

Dr. Brad Gustafson is an award-winning principal, best-selling author, and avid reader. He understands the critical role leaders play in creating the conditions where everyone in a school can be successful. Brad's approach to leadership is built on the belief that everything we do starts with relationships and connection. For additional support with literacy, leadership, or speaking needs, you can visit Brad's website, bradgustafson.com.

Dr. Mary Hemphill is a leadership expert and development coach, a K–16 educator and administrator, an author, and a motivational speaker. With over seventeen years of professional experience as a teacher, administrator, state director, and adjunct professor, Mary understands the importance of fusing education, empowerment, and leadership together as she works with learning and working communities and speaks to audiences across the country. She holds a PhD in Leadership Studies and has led, coached, and impacted close to forty thousand educational and corporate leaders around the world on transformational and innovative strategy, self-empowerment, and leadership development. Mary is the proud CEO and founder of The Limitless Leader™, an organization that helps people ignite the leader within them so they can better serve their community, company, and personal career through coaching, consulting, workshops, and keynotes aimed at corporate and educational leaders and organizations. Through her former roles as North Carolina's first state director of Computer Science and Technology Education, Director of Academics, and Chief Academic Officer, Mary is adept at working with leaders at every level to leverage support and leadership around strategic initiatives and programming as well as helping leaders navigate change management. Mary was named Regional Principal of the Year for the Sandhills Region of North Carolina for her transformational work in school turnaround and reform. You can connect with Mary on Instagram and X (@thelimitlesslady), or through her website, bealimitlessleader.com.

An author, artist, and leadership coach, **Mike Kleba** works as a public high school English, theater, and film teacher. Kleba is the coauthor of *Otherful: How to Change the World (and Your School) through Others*, a best-selling school leadership manual on how to develop greatness in others. He serves as cohost of the NYEdTech Meetup (the nation's largest) and sits on the SXSWEDU advisory board. He speaks at conferences around the world, including ASCD, EdTechX Europe, the National Charter School Conference, and SXSWEDU. He's done leadership work with the Gates Foundation, Google, Amazon, Microsoft, Columbia University, and the Library of Congress, among others. Interested in courage and vulnerability, he's run the NYC Marathon, gone hang-gliding in Brazil, been bungee jumping in New Zealand, and climbed Mt. Kilimanjaro. Follow him on all platforms (@mikekleba) and at Otherful.com.

Kari Lacny, an early child educator with a passion for shaping young minds, brings over twenty-six years of teaching experience to her classroom. For fifteen years, she dedicated herself to special education, fostering an inclusive and supportive environment for every student. Following this, she has spent eleven years as a dedicated kindergarten teacher, sparking a love for learning in countless young hearts. Armed with a master's degree in Reading Education, Kari is not just a teacher but a literacy advocate. Her expertise in reading education has empowered students to unlock the magic of words and stories. Currently residing in Zeeland, Michigan, Kari finds inspiration in the beauty of the Great Lakes state.

Abby Ramos Stanutz is an eighth-grade language and literature teacher in San Antonio, Texas. A graduate of Texas A&M University, she has spent the past twenty years teaching and promoting literacy in Title 1 schools across Texas. Known for her innovative and engaging lessons, she believes in empowering teachers to build rigorous, relevant learning experiences that honor the  students in their classrooms. She especially focuses on differentiating for gifted, special education, and emergent bilingual learners through free choice reading. An avid reader herself, she works to provide reading materials to underserved urban communities. She coaches, collaborates, and inspires teachers across the country through her regular TikTok PDs. Her viral Girltalk Club, a space for middle school girls, has been featured on educationweek.com and the *Friend Forward* podcast. She was San Antonio ISD's Distinguished Teacher of the Year and the KENS 5 Excel Award winner in 2023. See what she's reading on Instagram and Threads (@mrsramosstanutz) and get a peek at her latest lessons on TikTok (@abbyramosstanutz). She can be reached through her website, abbyramosstanutz.com.

CJ Reynolds has been a classroom educator for almost twenty years, teaching high school literature and the history of hip-hop in West Philadelphia, Pennsylvania, and Camden, New Jersey. He is also the author of *Teach Your Class Off* , the creator of the Real Rap with Reynolds YouTube channel, and a national speaker. Reynolds's work focuses on helping schools and their teachers become the educators they were meant to be by creating relevant, engaging, meaningful learning experiences that infuse playfulness, wonder, and fun to create classes that students *want* to be in. Reynolds's mission is to guide teachers on how to lead their classes with respect, boundaries, and accountability so they can continually be who their students *need* them to be.

Shane Saeed is a district instructional coach in Colorado working with K–12 educators. Currently, she is working on her doctoral degree in executive leadership with a focus on educational equity and is slated to defend her research in spring 2024. Shane's passion is sharing instructional practices with educators near and far. She facilitates professional development within her own

district, locally, and nationally and serves as a guest speaker and panelist at nearby universities. Shane was named as one of 20 Emerging Leaders for ASCD in 2022. Shane is a published author, and her book, *Be the Flame: Sparking Positive Classroom Communities*, is about how to build positive relationships and communities in different realms of education. She has also coauthored a structured morphology program for fourth- and fifth-grade teachers for her district. Shane continues to work in public education and to collaborate with teachers across the globe via her Instagram (@fantasticallyfourth), her podcast, *Vrain Waves*, her TikTok (@thefantasticallyfourth), and on X (@saeed_shane).

Vincent Taylor is an educator of twenty-nine years as well as a nationally acclaimed educational consultant. He has presented his

keynote, "If Instruction Isn't Engaging, I QUIT," to over sixty thousand educators in over fifteen school districts, eight national conferences, and five universities. Mr. Taylor is a graduate of the University of North Florida, where he received his BA in Elementary Education. His professional growth continued at the University of Florida. There he earned his master's degree in Curriculum and Instruction. Vincent has received numerous awards and recognition for his work, including the 2022 NAACP's Olivia Gay-Davis Education Award; the 2021 Literacy Is a Legacy Award; the 2020 Literacy Pros of Jacksonville Prestige Award; the 2012 Outstanding Graduate Leadership Award from the University of Florida; 2006 Teacher of the Year; 2005 Touching Hearts & Changing Lives Award from the Florida Association of School Social Workers, and a letter from Jacksonville mayor Alvin Brown for his Young Gentlemen's Club, a school-based mentoring group he founded in 1998. Mr. Taylor was nominated for the 2020 Image Award in Education Excellence. Mr. Taylor is proud to be a board member for the prestigious READ USA, Inc. organization. He is married to his lovely wife, Dina, and they have two beautiful daughters. Find out more about Vincent Taylor on X and YouTube @VinceTheWriter.

Taylor Teamann is a passionate new educator and graduate from Sam Houston State University. Out of college and into the real world, Taylor Teamann has embarked on a journey as a fifth-grade English teacher in Mabank, Texas. With determination and enthusiasm, Taylor Teamann dove headfirst into the world of education, shaping young minds and igniting a love for learning.

MORE FROM

IMPRESS

Empower
What Happens When Students Own Their Learning
by A.J. Juliani and John Spencer

Learner-Centered Innovation
Spark Curiosity, Ignite Passion, and Unleash Genius
by Katie Martin

Unleash Talent
Bringing Out the Best in Yourself and the Learners You Serve
by Kara Knollmeyer

Reclaiming Our Calling
Hold On to the Heart, Mind, and Hope of Education
by Brad Gustafson

Take the L.E.A.P.
Ignite a Culture of Innovation
by Elisabeth Bostwick

Drawn to Teach
An Illustrated Guide to Transforming Your Teaching
by Josh Stumpenhorst and illustrated by Trevor Guthke

Math Recess
Playful Learning in an Age of Disruption
by Sunil Singh and Dr. Christopher Brownell

Innovate inside the Box
Empowering Learners Through UDL and Innovator's Mindset
by George Couros and Katie Novak

Personal & Authentic
Designing Learning Experiences That Last a Lifetime
by Thomas C. Murray

Learner-Centered Leadership
A Blueprint for Transformational Change in Learning Communities
by Devin Vodicka

Kids These Days
A Game Plan for (Re)Connecting with Those We Teach, Lead, & Love
by Dr. Jody Carrington

UDL and Blended Learning
Thriving in Flexible Learning Landscapes
by Katie Novak and Catlin Tucker

Teachers These Days
Stories & Strategies for Reconnection
by Dr. Jody Carrington and Laurie McIntosh

Because of a Teacher
Stories of the Past to Inspire the Future of Education
written and curated by George Couros

Because of a Teacher, Volume 2
Stories from the First Years of Teaching
written and curated by George Couros

Evolving Education
Shifting to a Learner-Centered Paradigm
by Katie Martin

Adaptable
How to Create an Adaptable Curriculum and Flexible Learning Experiences That Work in Any Environment
by A.J. Juliani

Lead from Where You Are
Building Intention, Connection, and Direction in Our Schools
by Joe Sanfelippo

The Shift to Student-Led
Reimagining Classroom Workflows with UDL and Blended Learning
by Catlin R. Tucker and Katie Novak

The Design Thinking Classroom
Using Design Thinking to Reimagine the Role and Practice of Educators
by David Jakes

Made in the USA
Coppell, TX
07 June 2024

33227288R00118